FREE Test Taking Tips DVD Offer

To help us better serve you, we have developed a Test Taking Tips DVD that we would like to give you for FREE. **This DVD covers world-class test taking tips that you can use to be even more successful when you are taking your test.**

All that we ask is that you email us your feedback about your study guide. Please let us know what you thought about it – whether that is good, bad or indifferent.

To get your **FREE Test Taking Tips DVD**, email freedvd@studyguideteam.com with "FREE DVD" in the subject line and the following information in the body of the email:

     a. The title of your study guide.

     b. Your product rating on a scale of 1-5, with 5 being the highest rating.

     c. Your feedback about the study guide. What did you think of it?

     d. Your full name and shipping address to send your free DVD.

If you have any questions or concerns, please don't hesitate to contact us at freedvd@studyguideteam.com.

Thanks again!

AP Literature and Composition 2021 - 2022

AP English Literature and Composition Prep Book
with Practice Test Questions [2nd Edition]

Written and edited by TPB Publishing.

TPB Publishing is not associated with or endorsed by any official testing organization. TPB Publishing is a publisher of unofficial educational products. All test and organization names are trademarks of their respective owners. Content in this book is included for utilitarian purposes only and does not constitute an endorsement by TPB Publishing of any particular point of view.

Interested in buying more than 10 copies of our product? Contact us about bulk discounts: bulkorders@studyguideteam.com

ISBN 13: 9781628458794
ISBN 10: 1628458798

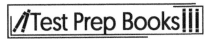

Table of Contents

Quick Overview

As you draw closer to taking your exam, effective preparation becomes more and more important. Thankfully, you have this study guide to help you get ready. Use this guide to help keep your studying on track and refer to it often.

This study guide contains several key sections that will help you be successful on your exam. The guide contains tips for what you should do the night before and the day of the test. Also included are test-taking tips. Knowing the right information is not always enough. Many well-prepared test takers struggle with exams. These tips will help equip you to accurately read, assess, and answer test questions.

A large part of the guide is devoted to showing you what content to expect on the exam and to helping you better understand that content. In this guide are practice test questions so that you can see how well you have grasped the content. Then, answer explanations are provided so that you can understand why you missed certain questions.

Don't try to cram the night before you take your exam. This is not a wise strategy for a few reasons. First, your retention of the information will be low. Your time would be better used by reviewing information you already know rather than trying to learn a lot of new information. Second, you will likely become stressed as you try to gain a large amount of knowledge in a short amount of time. Third, you will be depriving yourself of sleep. So be sure to go to bed at a reasonable time the night before. Being well-rested helps you focus and remain calm.

Be sure to eat a substantial breakfast the morning of the exam. If you are taking the exam in the afternoon, be sure to have a good lunch as well. Being hungry is distracting and can make it difficult to focus. You have hopefully spent lots of time preparing for the exam. Don't let an empty stomach get in the way of success!

When travelling to the testing center, leave earlier than needed. That way, you have a buffer in case you experience any delays. This will help you remain calm and will keep you from missing your appointment time at the testing center.

Be sure to pace yourself during the exam. Don't try to rush through the exam. There is no need to risk performing poorly on the exam just so you can leave the testing center early. Allow yourself to use all of the allotted time if needed.

Remain positive while taking the exam even if you feel like you are performing poorly. Thinking about the content you should have mastered will not help you perform better on the exam.

Once the exam is complete, take some time to relax. Even if you feel that you need to take the exam again, you will be well served by some down time before you begin studying again. It's often easier to convince yourself to study if you know that it will come with a reward!

Test-Taking Strategies

1. Predicting the Answer

When you feel confident in your preparation for a multiple-choice test, try predicting the answer before reading the answer choices. This is especially useful on questions that test objective factual knowledge. By predicting the answer before reading the available choices, you eliminate the possibility that you will be distracted or led astray by an incorrect answer choice. You will feel more confident in your selection if you read the question, predict the answer, and then find your prediction among the answer choices. After using this strategy, be sure to still read all of the answer choices carefully and completely. If you feel unprepared, you should not attempt to predict the answers. This would be a waste of time and an opportunity for your mind to wander in the wrong direction.

2. Reading the Whole Question

Too often, test takers scan a multiple-choice question, recognize a few familiar words, and immediately jump to the answer choices. Test authors are aware of this common impatience, and they will sometimes prey upon it. For instance, a test author might subtly turn the question into a negative, or he or she might redirect the focus of the question right at the end. The only way to avoid falling into these traps is to read the entirety of the question carefully before reading the answer choices.

3. Looking for Wrong Answers

Long and complicated multiple-choice questions can be intimidating. One way to simplify a difficult multiple-choice question is to eliminate all of the answer choices that are clearly wrong. In most sets of answers, there will be at least one selection that can be dismissed right away. If the test is administered on paper, the test taker could draw a line through it to indicate that it may be ignored; otherwise, the test taker will have to perform this operation mentally or on scratch paper. In either case, once the obviously incorrect answers have been eliminated, the remaining choices may be considered. Sometimes identifying the clearly wrong answers will give the test taker some information about the correct answer. For instance, if one of the remaining answer choices is a direct opposite of one of the eliminated answer choices, it may well be the correct answer. The opposite of obviously wrong is obviously right! Of course, this is not always the case. Some answers are obviously incorrect simply because they are irrelevant to the question being asked. Still, identifying and eliminating some incorrect answer choices is a good way to simplify a multiple-choice question.

4. Don't Overanalyze

Anxious test takers often overanalyze questions. When you are nervous, your brain will often run wild, causing you to make associations and discover clues that don't actually exist. If you feel that this may be a problem for you, do whatever you can to slow down during the test. Try taking a deep breath or counting to ten. As you read and consider the question, restrict yourself to the particular words used by the author. Avoid thought tangents about what the author *really* meant, or what he or she was *trying* to say. The only things that matter on a multiple-choice test are the words that are actually in the question. You must avoid reading too much into a multiple-choice question, or supposing that the writer meant something other than what he or she wrote.

5. No Need for Panic

It is wise to learn as many strategies as possible before taking a multiple-choice test, but it is likely that you will come across a few questions for which you simply don't know the answer. In this situation, avoid panicking. Because most multiple-choice tests include dozens of questions, the relative value of a single wrong answer is small. As much as possible, you should compartmentalize each question on a multiple-choice test. In other words, you should not allow your feelings about one question to affect your success on the others. When you find a question that you either don't understand or don't know how to answer, just take a deep breath and do your best. Read the entire question slowly and carefully. Try rephrasing the question a couple of different ways. Then, read all of the answer choices carefully. After eliminating obviously wrong answers, make a selection and move on to the next question.

6. Confusing Answer Choices

When working on a difficult multiple-choice question, there may be a tendency to focus on the answer choices that are the easiest to understand. Many people, whether consciously or not, gravitate to the answer choices that require the least concentration, knowledge, and memory. This is a mistake. When you come across an answer choice that is confusing, you should give it extra attention. A question might be confusing because you do not know the subject matter to which it refers. If this is the case, don't eliminate the answer before you have affirmatively settled on another. When you come across an answer choice of this type, set it aside as you look at the remaining choices. If you can confidently assert that one of the other choices is correct, you can leave the confusing answer aside. Otherwise, you will need to take a moment to try to better understand the confusing answer choice. Rephrasing is one way to tease out the sense of a confusing answer choice.

7. Your First Instinct

Many people struggle with multiple-choice tests because they overthink the questions. If you have studied sufficiently for the test, you should be prepared to trust your first instinct once you have carefully and completely read the question and all of the answer choices. There is a great deal of research suggesting that the mind can come to the correct conclusion very quickly once it has obtained all of the relevant information. At times, it may seem to you as if your intuition is working faster even than your reasoning mind. This may in fact be true. The knowledge you obtain while studying may be retrieved from your subconscious before you have a chance to work out the associations that support it. Verify your instinct by working out the reasons that it should be trusted.

8. Key Words

Many test takers struggle with multiple-choice questions because they have poor reading comprehension skills. Quickly reading and understanding a multiple-choice question requires a mixture of skill and experience. To help with this, try jotting down a few key words and phrases on a piece of scrap paper. Doing this concentrates the process of reading and forces the mind to weigh the relative importance of the question's parts. In selecting words and phrases to write down, the test taker thinks about the question more deeply and carefully. This is especially true for multiple-choice questions that are preceded by a long prompt.

9. Subtle Negatives

One of the oldest tricks in the multiple-choice test writer's book is to subtly reverse the meaning of a question with a word like *not* or *except*. If you are not paying attention to each word in the question, you can easily be led astray by this trick. For instance, a common question format is, "Which of the following is...?" Obviously, if the question instead is, "Which of the following is not...?," then the answer will be quite different. Even worse, the test makers are aware of the potential for this mistake and will include one answer choice that would be correct if the question were not negated or reversed. A test taker who misses the reversal will find what he or she believes to be a correct answer and will be so confident that he or she will fail to reread the question and discover the original error. The only way to avoid this is to practice a wide variety of multiple-choice questions and to pay close attention to each and every word.

10. Reading Every Answer Choice

It may seem obvious, but you should always read every one of the answer choices! Too many test takers fall into the habit of scanning the question and assuming that they understand the question because they recognize a few key words. From there, they pick the first answer choice that answers the question they believe they have read. Test takers who read all of the answer choices might discover that one of the latter answer choices is actually *more* correct. Moreover, reading all of the answer choices can remind you of facts related to the question that can help you arrive at the correct answer. Sometimes, a misstatement or incorrect detail in one of the latter answer choices will trigger your memory of the subject and will enable you to find the right answer. Failing to read all of the answer choices is like not reading all of the items on a restaurant menu: you might miss out on the perfect choice.

11. Spot the Hedges

One of the keys to success on multiple-choice tests is paying close attention to every word. This is never truer than with words like almost, most, some, and sometimes. These words are called "hedges" because they indicate that a statement is not totally true or not true in every place and time. An absolute statement will contain no hedges, but in many subjects, the answers are not always straightforward or absolute. There are always exceptions to the rules in these subjects. For this reason, you should favor those multiple-choice questions that contain hedging language. The presence of qualifying words indicates that the author is taking special care with his or her words, which is certainly important when composing the right answer. After all, there are many ways to be wrong, but there is only one way to be right! For this reason, it is wise to avoid answers that are absolute when taking a multiple-choice test. An absolute answer is one that says things are either all one way or all another. They often include words like *every*, *always*, *best*, and *never*. If you are taking a multiple-choice test in a subject that doesn't lend itself to absolute answers, be on your guard if you see any of these words.

12. Long Answers

In many subject areas, the answers are not simple. As already mentioned, the right answer often requires hedges. Another common feature of the answers to a complex or subjective question are qualifying clauses, which are groups of words that subtly modify the meaning of the sentence. If the question or answer choice describes a rule to which there are exceptions or the subject matter is complicated, ambiguous, or confusing, the correct answer will require many words in order to be expressed clearly and accurately. In essence, you should not be deterred by answer choices that seem excessively long. Oftentimes, the author of the text will not be able to write the correct answer without

offering some qualifications and modifications. Your job is to read the answer choices thoroughly and completely and to select the one that most accurately and precisely answers the question.

13. Restating to Understand

Sometimes, a question on a multiple-choice test is difficult not because of what it asks but because of how it is written. If this is the case, restate the question or answer choice in different words. This process serves a couple of important purposes. First, it forces you to concentrate on the core of the question. In order to rephrase the question accurately, you have to understand it well. Rephrasing the question will concentrate your mind on the key words and ideas. Second, it will present the information to your mind in a fresh way. This process may trigger your memory and render some useful scrap of information picked up while studying.

14. True Statements

Sometimes an answer choice will be true in itself, but it does not answer the question. This is one of the main reasons why it is essential to read the question carefully and completely before proceeding to the answer choices. Too often, test takers skip ahead to the answer choices and look for true statements. Having found one of these, they are content to select it without reference to the question above. Obviously, this provides an easy way for test makers to play tricks. The savvy test taker will always read the entire question before turning to the answer choices. Then, having settled on a correct answer choice, he or she will refer to the original question and ensure that the selected answer is relevant. The mistake of choosing a correct-but-irrelevant answer choice is especially common on questions related to specific pieces of objective knowledge. A prepared test taker will have a wealth of factual knowledge at his or her disposal and should not be careless in its application.

15. No Patterns

One of the more dangerous ideas that circulates about multiple-choice tests is that the correct answers tend to fall into patterns. These erroneous ideas range from a belief that B and C are the most common right answers, to the idea that an unprepared test-taker should answer "A-B-A-C-A-D-A-B-A." It cannot be emphasized enough that pattern-seeking of this type is exactly the WRONG way to approach a multiple-choice test. To begin with, it is highly unlikely that the test maker will plot the correct answers according to some predetermined pattern. The questions are scrambled and delivered in a random order. Furthermore, even if the test maker was following a pattern in the assignation of correct answers, there is no reason why the test taker would know which pattern he or she was using. Any attempt to discern a pattern in the answer choices is a waste of time and a distraction from the real work of taking the test. A test taker would be much better served by extra preparation before the test than by reliance on a pattern in the answers.

FREE DVD OFFER

Don't forget that doing well on your exam includes both understanding the test content and understanding how to use what you know to do well on the test. We offer a completely FREE Test Taking Tips DVD that covers world class test taking tips that you can use to be even more successful when you are taking your test.

All that we ask is that you email us your feedback about your study guide. To get your **FREE Test Taking Tips DVD**, email freedvd@studyguideteam.com with "FREE DVD" in the subject line and the following information in the body of the email:

- The title of your study guide.
- Your product rating on a scale of 1-5, with 5 being the highest rating.
- Your feedback about the study guide. What did you think of it?
- Your full name and shipping address to send your free DVD.

Introduction

Function of the Test

The Advanced Placement (AP) English Literature and Composition Exam, created by the College Board, is an exam designed to offer college placement for high school students. The AP program allows students to earn college credit, advanced placement, or both, through the program's offering of the course and end-of-course exam. Sometimes universities may also look at AP scores to determine college admission. This guide gives an overview of the exam along with a condensed version of what might be taught in the AP English Literature and Composition course.

The AP program creates multiple versions of each AP exam to be administered within various U.S. geographic regions. With these exams, schools can offer late testing and discourage sharing questions across time zones. The AP exam is given in the U.S. nationwide; and outside of Canada and the U.S., credits are only sometimes accepted in other countries. The College Board website has a list of universities outside of the U.S. that recognize AP for credit and admission.

In 2018, 404,014 students took the AP English Literature and Composition exam.

Test Administration

On their website, the College Board provides a specific day that the AP English Literature and Composition exam is given. For example, in 2020, the AP English Literature and Composition exam is given on Wednesday, May 6, 2020, at 8 a.m. Coordinators should notify students when and where to report.

Students may take the exam again if they are not happy with their results. However, since the exam is given one day per year, students must wait until the following year to retake the exam. Both scores will be reported unless the student cancels or withholds one of the scores.

A wide range of accommodations are available to students who live with disabilities. Students will work with their school to request accommodations. If students or parents do not request accommodations through their school, disabilities must be appropriately documented and requested in advance via the College Board website.

Test Format

The AP Literature and Composition exam is three hours long and contains a multiple-choice section and a free-response section. The multiple-choice section is made up of reading passages from fiction, nonfiction, and poetry, and has fifty-five questions total. This section takes up 45 percent of the exam and lasts sixty minutes. The free-response section has three questions: a poetry analysis, a prose fiction analysis, and a literary argument. This section takes up 55 percent of the exam and lasts for two hours. The exam relies on a variety of time periods; students are expected to be familiar with canonized literature throughout history.

The exam tests on literary elements such as character, setting, structure, narration, figurative language, and literary argumentation.

Scoring

Scoring on the AP exam is similar to that of a college course. The table below shows an outline of scores and what they mean:

Score	Recommendation	College Grade
5	Extremely well qualified	A
4	Well qualified	A-, B+,B
3	Qualified	B-,C+,C
2	Possibly qualified	n/a
1	No recommendation	n/a

While multiple-choice questions are graded via machine, the free-response questions are graded by AP Readers. Scores on the free-response section are weighted and combined with the scores from the multiple-choice questions. The raw score from these two sections is converted into a 1–5 scale, as explained in the table above. The multiple-choice section is 45 percent of the exam grade, and the free-response section is 55 percent of the exam grade.

Colleges are responsible for setting their own criteria for placement and admissions, so check with specific universities to assess their criteria concerning the AP exam.

Recent/Future Developments

In the 2019/2020 year, changes were made to how the free-response questions are scored, which are now on a six-point analytic scale instead of on a nine-point scale:

- Claim and thesis: one point
- Evidence to develop the claim: four points
- Sophistication of the argument: one point

Additionally, the breakdown of the exam changed. Instead of 50 percent designated to texts pre-twentieth century, the breakdown is now the following:

- 25 percent pre-twentieth century
- 50 percent twentieth century
- 25 percent contemporary (2000s to present)

For the free-response questions, note the following:

- Translated works will not be listed on free-response question #3, but students will be allowed to choose a translated work to write about if they wish.
- For free-response question #3, literary nonfiction is now acceptable to write about.

Finally, the updated exam focuses on the skill of the test taker to examine the narrator/speaker and what their function is in the text.

English Literature

Literary Works and Literary Contexts

Major Literary Works

The AP English Literature and Composition assumes test takers will have a familiarity with a wide range of American, British, World, and Young Adult literary works. In most cases, the test taker will be presented with a quoted literary passage and be required to answer one or more questions about it. This may involve having to identify the literary work presented from a list of options.

The ability of the test taker to demonstrate familiarity of major literary works is key in success when taking AP exams. The following chart offers some examples of major works in addition to those listed elsewhere in this guide, but the list is not exhaustive.

<u>American</u>
Fictional Prose

Harriet Beecher Stowe | *Uncle Tom's Cabin*
Ernest Hemingway | *For Whom the Bell Tolls*
Jack London | *The Call of the Wild*
Toni Morrison | *Beloved*
N. Scott Momaday | *The Way to Rainy Mountain*
J.D. Salinger | *Catcher in the Rye*
John Steinbeck | *Grapes of Wrath*
Alice Walker | *The Color Purple*

Drama

Edward Albee | *Who's Afraid of Virginia Woolf?*
Lorraine Hansberry | *A Raisin in the Sun*
Amiri Baraka | *Dutchman*
Eugene O'Neill |*Long Day's Journey into Night*
Sam Shephard | *Buried Child*
Thornton Wilder I *Our Town*
Tennessee Williams | *A Streetcar Named Desire*

Poetry

Anne Bradstreet | "In Reference to her Children, 23 June 1659"
Emily Dickinson | "Because I could not stop for Death"
Sylvia Plath | "Mirror"
Langston Hughes | "Harlem"
Edgar Allen Poe | "The Raven"
Phillis Wheatley | "On Being Brought from Africa to America"
Walt Whitman | "Song of Myself"

Literary Non-fiction

Maya Angelou | *I Know Why the Caged Bird Sings*
Truman | *Capote In Cold Blood*

9

Frederick Douglass | *My Bondage and My Freedom*
Archie Fire | *Lame Deer The Gift of Power: The Life and Teachings of a Lakota Medicine Man*
Helen Keller | *The Story of My Life*
Dave Pelzer | *A Child Called "It"*

British
Fictional Prose

John Bunyan | *The Pilgrim's Progress*
Joseph Conrad | *Heart of Darkness*
Charles Dickens | *Tale of Two Cities*
George Eliot | *Middlemarch*
George Orwell | *1984*
Mary Shelley | *Frankenstein*

Drama

Samuel Beckett | *Waiting for Godot*
Caryl Churchill | *Top Girls*
William Congreve | *The Way of the World*
Michael Frayn | *Noises Off*
William Shakespeare | *Macbeth*
Oscar Wilde | *The Importance of Being Earnest*

Poetry

Elizabeth Barrett Browning | "How Do I Love Thee? (Sonnet 43)"
Robert Burns | "A Red, Red Rose"
Samuel Taylor Coleridge | "Rime of the Ancient Mariner"
T.S. Eliot | "Love Song of J. Alfred Prufrock"
John Milton | "Paradise Lost"

Literary Non-fiction

Vera Brittain | *Testament of Youth*
T. E. Lawrence | *Seven Pillars of Wisdom*
Doris Lessing | *Going Home*
Brian Blessed | *Absolute Pandemonium: The Autobiography*
Virginia Woolf | *A Room of One's Own*

World

Fictional Prose

Anonymous | *The Epic of Gilgamesh*
Chinua Achebe | *Things Fall Apart*
Margaret Atwood | *The Handmaid's Tale*
Pearl S. Buck | *The Good Earth*
Miguel de Cervantes | *Don Quixote*
Fyodor Dostoyevsky | *Crime and Punishment*
Gabriel Garcia Marquez | *One Hundred Years of Solitude*
James Joyce | *Ulysses*
Nikos Kazantzakis | *Zorba the Greek*
Boris Pasternak | *Dr. Zhivago*
Amy Tan | *The Joy Luck Club*
Voltaire | *Candide*

Drama

Bertolt Brecht | *Mother Courage and her Children*
Anton Chekhov | *The Seagull*
Lady Gregory | *Workhouse Ward*
Henrik Ibsen | *A Doll's House*
Luigi Pirandello | *Six Characters in Search of an Author*
Molière | *Tartuffe*
Sophocles | *Antigone*
August Strindberg | *Miss Julie*
Vyasa | *The Bhagavad Gita*
Johann Wolfgang von Goethe | *Faust*

Poetry

Anonymous | *Beowulf*
Anonymous | *The Ramayana*
Dante Alighieri | *The Divine Comedy*
Federico García Lorca | *Gypsy Ballads*
Omar Khayyám | *The Rubaiyat*
Kahlil Gibran | *The Prophet*
Andrew Barton "Banjo" Paterson | "Waltzing Matilda"
Taslima Nasrin | *"Character"*
Kostis Palamas | "Ancient Eternal And Immortal Spirit"
Maria Elena Cruz Varela | "Kaleidoscope"
King David | The 23rd Psalm, the Judeo-Christian Bible

Literary Non-fiction

Pavel Basinsky | *Flight from Paradise*
Jung Chang | *Wild Swans*
Confucius | *The Analects of Confucius*
Viktor Frankl | *Man's Search for Meaning*
Mahatma Gandhi | *India of my Dreams*
Nelson Mandela | *Long Walk to Freedom*
Fatema Mernissi | *Beyond the Veil*

Jonathan Swift | "A Modest Proposal"
Mythology

Homer | *The Iliad*
Homer | *The Odyssey*
Hesiod | *Theogony*
Ovid | *Metamorphoses*
Virgil | *Aeneid*
Valmiki | *Ramayana*
Vyasa | *Bhagavad Gita*
Epic of Gilgamesh
Ferdowsi | The Shahnameh
Anonymous | *Beowulf*
Anonymous | The Volsunga Saga

Young Adult

Fictional Prose

Jodi Lynn Anderson | *Tiger Lily*
Lois Lowry | *The Giver*
Scott O'Dell | *Island of the Blue Dolphins*
Katherine Paterson Jacob | *Have I Loved*
Antoine de Saint-Exupéry | *The Little Prince*
Ellen Raskin | *The Westing Game*
P. L. Travers | *Mary Poppins*
Marcus Zusak | *The Book Thief*
Drama

Peter Dee | *Voices from the High School*
William Gibson | *The Miracle Worker*
Poetry

Sandra Cisneros | "Eleven"
Eamon Grennan | "Cat Scat"
Tom Junod | "My Mother Couldn't Cook"
Tupac Shakur | "The Rose that Grew from Concrete"
Literary Non-fiction

Sherman Alexie | *The Absolutely True Diary of a Part-Time Indian*
Anne Frank | *The Diary of Anne Frank*
Philip Hoose | *The Boys who Challenged Hitler*
Cynthia Levinson | *We've Got a Job*
Malala Yousafzai and Christina Lamb | *I am Malala*

Literary Contexts

Understanding that works of literature emerged either because of a particular context—or perhaps despite a context—is key to analyzing them effectively.

Historical Context

The **historical context** of a piece of literature can refer to the time period, setting, or conditions of living at the time it was written as well as the context of the work. For example, Hawthorne's *The Scarlet Letter* was published in 1850, though the setting of the story is 1642–1649. Historically, then, when Hawthorne wrote his novel, the United States found itself at odds as the beginnings of a potential Civil War were in view. Thus, the historical context is potentially significant as it pertains to the ideas of traditions and values, which Hawthorne addresses in his story of Hester Prynne in the era of Puritanism.

Cultural Context

The **cultural context** of a piece of literature refers to cultural factors, such as the beliefs, religions, and customs that surround a work of literature. The Puritan's beliefs, religion, and customs in Hawthorne's novel are significant because they are at the core of the plot—the reason Hester wears the "A" and why Arthur kills himself. The customs of people in the Antebellum Period, though not quite as restrictive, were still somewhat similar. This would impact how the audience of the time received the novel.

Literary Context

Literary context refers to the consideration of the genre, potentially at the time the work was written. In 1850, Realism and Romanticism were the driving forces in literature in the U.S., with depictions of life as it was at the time in which the work was written (Realism) as well as content describing the beauty of nature (Romanticism). Thus, an audience in Hawthorne's time would have been well satisfied with the elements of both offered in the text. They would have been looking for details about everyday things and people (Realism), but they also would appreciate his approach to description of nature and the focus on the individual (American Romanticism). The contexts would be significant as they would pertain to evaluating the work against those criteria.

Here are some questions to use when considering context:

- When was the text written?
- What was society like at the time the text was written, or what was it like, given the work's identified time period?
- Who or what influenced the writer?
- What political or social influences might there have been?
- What influences may there have been in the genre that may have affected the writer?

Additionally, test takers should familiarize themselves with literary periods such as Old and Middle English, American Colonial, American Renaissance, American Naturalistic, and British and American Modernist and Post-Modernist movements. Most students of literature will have had extensive exposure to these literary periods in history, and while it is not necessary to recognize every major literary work on sight and associate that work to its corresponding movement or cultural context, the test taker should be familiar enough with the historical and cultural significance of each test passage in order to be able to address test questions correctly.

The following brief description of some literary contexts and their associated literary examples follows. It is not an all-inclusive list. The test taker should read each description, then follow up with independent study to clarify each movement, its context, its most familiar authors, and their works.

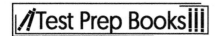

Literary Movements

Metaphysical Poetry

Metaphysical poetry is the descriptor applied to 17th century poets whose poetry emphasized the lyrical quality of their work. These works contain highly creative poetic conceits or metaphoric comparisons between two highly dissimilar things or ideas. Metaphysical poetry is characterized by highly prosaic language and complicated, often layered, metaphor.

Poems such as John Donne's "The Flea," Andrew Marvell's "To His Coy Mistress," George Herbert's "The Collar," Henry Vaughan's "The World," and Richard Crashaw's "A Song" are associated with this type of poetry.

British Romanticism

British Romanticism was a cultural and literary movement within Europe that developed at the end of the 18th century and extended into the 19th century. It occurred partly in response to aristocratic, political, and social norms and partly in response to the Industrial Revolution of the day. Characterized by intense emotion, major literary works of British Romanticism embrace the idea of aestheticism and the beauty of nature. Literary works exalted folk customs and historical art and encouraged spontaneity of artistic endeavor. The movement embraced the heroic ideal and the concept that heroes would raise the quality of society.

Authors who are classified as British Romantics include Samuel Taylor Coleridge, John Keats, George Byron, Mary Shelley, Percy Bysshe Shelley, and William Blake. Well-known works include Samuel Taylor Coleridge's "Kubla Khan," John Keats' "Ode on a Grecian Urn," George Byron's "Childe Harold's Pilgrimage," Mary Shelley's *Frankenstein*, Percy Bysshe Shelley's "Ode to the West Wind," and William Blake's "The Tyger."

American Romanticism

American Romanticism occurred within the American literary scene beginning early in the 19th century. While many aspects were similar to British Romanticism, American Romanticism is characterized as having gothic aspects and as well as individualistic aspects. It also embraced the concept of the *noble savage*—the idea that indigenous culture uncorrupted by civilization is better than advanced society.

Well-known authors and works include Nathanial Hawthorne's *The House of the Seven Gables*, Edgar Allan Poe's "The Raven" and "The Cask of Amontillado," Emily Dickinson's "I Felt a Funeral in My Brain" and James Fenimore Cooper's *The Last of the Mohicans*.

Transcendentalism

Transcendentalism was a movement that applied to a way of thinking that developed within the United States, specifically New England, around 1836. While this way of thinking originally employed philosophical aspects, transcendentalism spread to all forms of art, literature, and even lifestyle. It was born out of a reaction to traditional rationalism and purported concepts such as a higher divinity, feminism, humanitarianism, and communal living. Transcendentalism valued intuition, self-reliance, and the idea that human nature was inherently good.

Well-known authors include Ralph Waldo Emerson, Henry David Thoreau, Louisa May Alcott, and Ellen Sturgis Hooper. Works include Ralph Waldo Emerson's "Self-Reliance" and "Uriel," Henry David Thoreau's *Walden* and *Civil Disobedience*, Louisa May Alcott's *Little Women*, and Ellen Sturgis Hooper's "I Slept, and Dreamed that Life was Beauty."

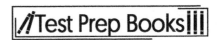

Harlem Renaissance

The **Harlem Renaissance** is the descriptor given to the cultural, artistic, and social boom that developed in Harlem, New York, at the beginning of the 20th century, spanning the 1920s and 1930s. Originally termed *The New Negro Movement*, it emphasized African-American urban cultural expression and migration across the United States. It had strong roots in African-American Christianity, discourse, and intellectualism. The Harlem Renaissance heavily influenced the development of music and fashion as well. Its singular characteristic was to embrace Pan-American culturalisms; however, strong themes of the slavery experience and African-American folk traditions also emerged. A hallmark of the Harlem Renaissance was that it laid the foundation for the future Civil Rights Movement in the United States.

Well-known authors and works include Zora Neale Hurston's *Their Eyes Were Watching God*, Richard Wright's *Native Son*, Langston Hughes' "I, Too," and James Weldon Johnson's "God's Trombones: Seven Negro Sermons in Verse" and *The Book of American Negro Poetry*.

Young Adult Literature

Young Adult (YA) Literature is aimed at readers who are thirteen years of age or older. As such, it should be appropriate to the age and interest level of its intended readers. Young Adult novels tend to deal with more mature themes such as sex, drinking, and death, and may also use profanity. Young Adult literature is not limited to any one genre, with popular novels running the gamut from fantasy to historical fiction. The YA novel typically features a teen protagonist who faces real issues that a teen might face. Adults are included in YA novels, but usually as secondary characters to the teen protagonist; typically, in such novels, the teen protagonist may need to face or stand up to an adult.

Six Big Ideas

Character

Characters are the story's figures that assume primary, secondary, or minor roles. Central or major characters are those integral to the story—the plot cannot be resolved without them. A central character can be a **protagonist**, or hero. There may be more than one protagonist, and they don't always have to possess good characteristics. A character can also be an **antagonist**—the force against a protagonist.

Dynamic characters change over the course of the plot time. **Static characters** do not change. A **symbolic character** is one that represents an author's idea about society in general—e.g., Napoleon in Orwell's *Animal Farm*. **Stock characters** are those that appear across genres and embrace stereotypes—e.g., the cowboy of the Wild West or the blonde bombshell in a detective novel. A **flat character** is one that does not present a lot of complexity or depth, while a **rounded character** does. Sometimes, the narrator of a story or the speaker in a poem can be a character—e.g., Nick Carraway in F. Scott Fitzgerald's *The Great Gatsby* or the speaker in Robert Browning's "My Last Duchess." The narrator might also function as a character in prose, though not be part of the story—e.g., Charles Dickens' narrator of *A Christmas Carol*.

Point of View

The **point of view** is the position the narrator takes when telling the story in prose. If a narrator is incorporated in a drama, the point of view may vary; in poetry, point of view refers to the position the speaker takes in a poem.

First Person

The first-person point-of-view is when the writer uses the word "I" in the text. Poetry often uses first person, e.g., William Wordsworth's "I Wandered Lonely as a Cloud." Two examples of prose written in first person are Suzanne Collins' *The Hunger Games* and Anthony Burgess's *A Clockwork Orange*.

Second Person

The second-person point-of-view is when the writer uses the pronoun "you." It is not widely used in prose fiction, but as a technique, it has been used by writers such as William Faulkner in *Absalom, Absalom!* and Albert Camus in *The Fall*. It is more common in poetry—e.g., Pablo Neruda's "If You Forget Me."

Third Person

Third-person point-of-view is when the writer utilizes pronouns such as him, her, or them. It may be the most utilized point-of-view in prose, as it provides flexibility to an author and is the one with which readers are most familiar. There are three main types of third person used:

- **Third-person limited point-of-view** refers to a story told by a narrator who has access to the thoughts and feelings of just one character.

- In **third-person omniscient point-of-view**, the narrator has access to the thoughts and feelings of all the characters.

- In **third-person objective point-of-view**, the narrator is like a fly on the wall and can see and hear what the characters do and say but does not have access to their thoughts and feelings.

Understanding Relationships

Inferences are useful in gaining a deeper understanding of how people, events, and ideas are connected in a passage. Readers can use the same strategies used with general inferences and analyzing texts—paying attention to details and using them to make reasonable guesses about the text—to read between the lines and get a more complete picture of how (and why) characters are thinking, feeling, and acting. Read the following passage from O. Henry's story "The Gift of the Magi":

> One dollar and eighty-seven cents. That was all. And sixty cents of it was in pennies. Pennies saved one and two at a time by bulldozing the grocer and the vegetable man and the butcher until one's cheeks burned with the silent imputation of parsimony that such close dealing implied. Three times Della counted it. One dollar and eighty-seven cents. And the next day would be Christmas.

> There was clearly nothing to do but flop down on the shabby little couch and howl. So Della did it.

These paragraphs introduce the reader to the character Della. Even though the author doesn't include a direct description of Della, the reader can already form a general impression of her personality and emotions. One detail that should stick out to the reader is repetition: "one dollar and eighty-seven cents." This amount is repeated twice in the first paragraph, along with other descriptions of money: "sixty cents of it was in pennies," "pennies saved one and two at a time." The story's preoccupation with money parallels how Della herself is constantly thinking about her finances—"three times Della counted" her meager savings. Already the reader can guess that Della is having money problems. Next, think about her emotions. The first paragraph describes haggling over groceries "until one's cheeks

burned"—another way to describe blushing. People tend to blush when they are embarrassed or ashamed, so readers can infer that Della is ashamed by her financial situation. This inference is also supported by the second paragraph, when she flops down and howls on her "shabby little couch." Clearly, she's in distress. Without saying, "Della has no money and is embarrassed to be poor," O. Henry is able to communicate the same impression to readers through his careful inclusion of details.

A character's **motive** is their reason for acting a certain way. Usually, characters are motivated by something that they want. In the passage above, why is Della upset about not having enough money? There's an important detail at the end of the first paragraph: "the next day would be Christmas." Why is money especially important around Christmas? Christmas is a holiday when people exchange gifts. If Della is struggling with money, she's probably also struggling to buy gifts. So a shrewd reader should be able to guess that Della's motivation is wanting to buy a gift for someone—but she's currently unable to afford it, leading to feelings of shame and frustration.

In order to understand characters in a text, readers should keep the following questions in mind:

- What words does the author use to describe the character? Are these words related to any specific emotions or personality traits (for example, characteristics like rude, friendly, unapproachable, or innocent)?

- What does the character say? Does their dialogue seem to be straightforward, or are they hiding some thoughts or emotions?

- What actions can be observed from this character? How do their actions reflect their feelings?

- What does the character want? What do they do to get it?

Setting

The **setting** is the time, place, or set of surroundings in which the story occurs. It includes time or time span, place(s), climates, geography—man-made or natural—or cultural environments. Emily Dickinson's poem "Because I could not stop for Death" has a simple setting—the narrator's symbolic ride with Death through town towards the local graveyard. Conversely, Leo Tolstoy's *War and Peace* encompasses numerous settings within settings in the areas affected by the Napoleonic Wars, spanning 1805 to 1812.

Context Clues

Knowledge of synonyms and antonyms is crucial for writing and identifying a good paraphrase and also helps readers expand their mental vocabulary network. Another useful vocabulary skill is being able to understand meaning in context. A word's **context** refers to all the other words and information surrounding it, and the context of a word can have an impact on how readers interpret that word's meaning. Of course, many words have more than one definition. For example, consider the meaning of the word *engaged*. The first definition that comes to mind might be "promised to be married," but consider the following sentences:

A: The two armies engaged in a conflict that lasted all night.

B: The three-hour lecture flew by because students were so engaged in the material.

C: The busy executive engaged a new assistant to help with his workload.

As you can see, *engaged* has a variety of other meanings. In these sentences, respectively, it can mean: "battled," "interested or involved," and "appointed or employed." With so many possible definitions, readers may wonder how to decide which one to apply in a given sentence. The appropriate meaning is prioritized based on context. For example, sentence *C* mentions "executive," "assistant," and "workload," so readers can assume that *engaged* has something to do with work—in which case, "appointed or employed" would be the best definition for this context. Context clues can also be found in sentence *A*. Words like "armies" and "conflicts" show that this sentence is about a military situation (and not about marriage or the office), so in this context, *engaged* is closest in meaning to "battled." By using context clues—the surrounding words in the sentence—readers can easily select the most appropriate definition for the word in question.

In addition to helping readers select the best meaning for a word with many definitions, context clues can also help readers when they don't know any meanings for a certain word. Test writers will deliberately ask about vocabulary that test takers are probably unfamiliar with in order to measure their ability to use context to make an educated guess about a word's meaning.

Which of the following is the closest in meaning to the word *loquacious* in the following sentence?

The loquacious professor was notorious for always taking too long to finish his lectures.
   a. Knowledgeable
   b. Enthusiastic
   c. Approachable
   d. Talkative
   e. Inexperienced

Even if the word *loquacious* seems completely new, it is still possible to utilize context to make a good guess about the word's meaning. Grammatically, it is apparent that *loquacious* is an adjective that modifies the noun "professor"—so l*oquacious* must be some kind of quality or characteristic. A clue in this sentence is "taking too long to finish his lectures." Readers should then brainstorm qualities that might cause a professor to be late. Perhaps he is "disorganized," "slow," or "talkative"—all words that might still make sense in this sentence. After brainstorming some ideas for the word's definition, take a look at the choices for the question. Choice *D* matches one word from the brainstorming session, and it is a logical choice for this sentence—the professor talks too much, so his lectures run late. In fact, *loquacious* means "talkative" or "wordy."

One way to use context clues is to think of potential replacement words before considering the answer choices given in the question. However, if it is truly a struggle to come up with any possibilities, turn to the answer choices first and try to replace each of them in the sentence to see if the sentence is still logical and retains the same meaning.

Which of the following is the closest in meaning to the word *dogma* in the following sentence?

Martin Luther was a revolutionary religious figure because he argued against Catholic dogma and encouraged a new interpretation of Christianity.
   a. Punishments
   b. Doctrines
   c. Leadership
   d. Procedures
   e. History

Based on context, this sentence has something to do with religious conflict and interpretations of Christian faith. The only word related to religious belief is Choice *B*, *doctrines*, which is in fact the best synonym for *dogma*.

Yet another way to use context clues is to consider clues in the word itself. Most students are probably familiar with prefixes, suffixes, and root words—the building blocks of many English words. A little knowledge goes a long way when it comes to these components of English vocabulary, and they can point readers in the right direction when they need help finding an appropriate definition.

Which of the following is the closest in meaning to the word *antipathy* in the following sentence?

A strong antipathy existed between Margaret and her new neighbor, Susan.
    a. Enmity
    b. Resemblance
    c. Relationship
    d. Alliance
    e. Persuasion

In this case, the sentence does not provide much context for the word *antipathy*. However, the word itself gives some useful clues. The prefix *anti-* means "opposite or against," so *antipathy* probably has a negative meaning. Also, if readers already know words like "sympathy" or "empathy," they might guess that the root word "path" is related to emotions. So, *antipathy* must be a feeling *against* something. *Alliance* is a positive connection, *relationship* is too neutral, and *resemblance* means two things are similar to each other. *Persuasion* usually relates to a set of beliefs or the act of coercing someone of something, so this is choice is nonsensical for the provided sentences. The only word that shows a negative or opposite feeling is Choice *A*, enmity (the feeling of being enemies). In this way, even an unfamiliar word may contain clues that can indicate its meaning.

Structure

Authors' Intent with Text Structure

When it comes to an author's writing, readers should always identify a position or stance. No matter how objective a text may seem, readers should assume the author has preconceived beliefs. One can reduce the likelihood of accepting an invalid argument by looking for multiple articles on the topic, including those with varying opinions. If several opinions point in the same direction and are backed by reputable peer-reviewed sources, it's more likely the author has a valid argument. Positions that run contrary to widely held beliefs and existing data should invite scrutiny. There are exceptions to the rule, so be a careful consumer of information.

Though themes, symbols, and motifs are buried deep within the text and can sometimes be difficult to infer, an author's purpose is usually obvious from the beginning. There are four purposes of writing: to inform, to persuade, to describe, and to entertain. Informative writing presents facts in an accessible way. Persuasive writing appeals to emotions and logic to inspire the reader to adopt a specific stance. Be wary of this type of writing, as it can mask a lack of objectivity with powerful emotion. Descriptive writing is designed to paint a picture in the reader's mind, while texts that entertain are often narratives designed to engage and delight the reader.

The various writing styles are usually blended, with one purpose dominating the rest. A persuasive text, for example, might begin with a humorous tale to make readers more receptive to the persuasive message, or a recipe in a cookbook designed to inform might be preceded by an entertaining anecdote that makes the recipes more appealing.

Topic Versus the Main Idea

It is important to know the difference between the topic and the main idea of the text. Even though these two are similar because they both present the central point of a text, they have distinctive differences. A **topic** is the subject of the text; it can usually be described in a one- to two-word phrase and appears in the simplest form. On the other hand, the **main idea** is more detailed and provides the author's central point of the text. It can be expressed through a complete sentence and is often found in the beginning, middle, or end of a paragraph. In most nonfiction books, the first sentence of the passage usually (but not always) states the main idea

Review the passage below to explore the topic versus the main idea:

> Cheetahs are one of the fastest mammals on the land, reaching up to 70 miles an hour over short distances. Even though cheetahs can run as fast as 70 miles an hour, they usually only have to run half that speed to catch up with their choice of prey. Cheetahs cannot maintain a fast pace over long periods of time because their bodies will overheat. After a chase, cheetahs need to rest for approximately 30 minutes prior to eating or returning to any other activity.

In the example above, the topic of the passage is "Cheetahs" simply because that is the subject of the text. The main idea of the text is "Cheetahs are one of the fastest mammals on the land but can only maintain a fast pace for shorter distances." While it covers the topic, it is more detailed and refers to the text in its entirety. The text continues to provide additional details called supporting details.

Supporting Details

Supporting details help readers better develop and understand the main idea. Supporting details answer questions like *who, what, where, when, why,* and *how*. Different types of supporting details include examples, facts and statistics, anecdotes, and sensory details.

Persuasive and informative texts often use supporting details. In persuasive texts, authors attempt to make readers agree with their points of view, and supporting details are often used as "selling points." If authors make a statement, they need to support the statement with evidence in order to adequately persuade readers. Informative texts use supporting details such as examples and facts to inform readers. Review the previous "Cheetahs" passage to find examples of supporting details.

> Cheetahs are one of the fastest mammals on the land, reaching up to 70 miles an hour over short distances. Even though cheetahs can run as fast as 70 miles an hour, they usually only have to run half that speed to catch up with their choice of prey. Cheetahs cannot maintain a fast pace over long periods of time because their bodies will overheat. After a chase, cheetahs need to rest for approximately 30 minutes prior to eating or returning to any other activity.

In the example, supporting details include:

- Cheetahs reach up to 70 miles per hour over short distances.
- They usually only have to run half that speed to catch up with their prey.
- Cheetahs will overheat if they exert a high speed over longer distances.
- Cheetahs need to rest for 30 minutes after a chase.

Look at the diagram below (applying the cheetah example) to help determine the hierarchy of topic, main idea, and supporting details.

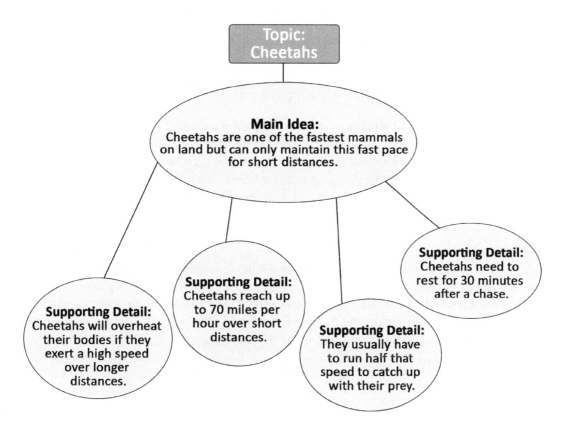

Development of Themes

Theme or Central Message

The **theme** is the central message of a fictional work, whether that work is structured as prose, drama, or poetry. It is the heart of what an author is trying to say to readers through the writing, and theme is largely conveyed through literary elements and techniques.

In literature, a theme can often be determined by considering the overarching narrative conflict with the work. Though there are several types of conflicts and several potential themes within them, the following are the most common:

- **Individual against the self**—relevant to themes of self-awareness, internal struggles, pride, coming of age, facing reality, fate, free will, vanity, loss of innocence, loneliness, isolation, fulfillment, failure, and disillusionment

- **Individual against nature**—relevant to themes of knowledge vs. ignorance, nature as beauty, quest for discovery, self-preservation, chaos and order, circle of life, death, and destruction of beauty

- **Individual against society**—relevant to themes of power, beauty, good, evil, war, class struggle, totalitarianism, role of men/women, wealth, corruption, change vs. tradition, capitalism, destruction, heroism, injustice, and racism

- **Individual against another individual**—relevant to themes of hope, loss of love or hope, sacrifice, power, revenge, betrayal, and honor

For example, in Hawthorne's *The Scarlet Letter*, one possible narrative conflict could be the individual against the self, with a relevant theme of internal struggles. This theme is alluded to through characterization—Dimmesdale's moral struggle with his love for Hester and Hester's internal struggles with the truth and her daughter, Pearl. It's also alluded to through plot—Dimmesdale's suicide and Hester helping the very townspeople who initially condemned her.

Sometimes, a text can convey a **message** or **universal lesson**—a truth or insight that the reader infers from the text, based on analysis of the literary and/or poetic elements. This message is often presented as a statement. For example, a potential message in Shakespeare's *Hamlet* could be "Revenge is what ultimately drives the human soul." This message can be immediately determined through plot and characterization in numerous ways, but it can also be determined through the setting of Norway, which is bordering on war.

How Authors Develop Theme

Authors employ a variety of techniques to present a theme. They may compare or contrast characters, events, places, ideas, or historical or invented settings to speak thematically. They may use analogies, metaphors, similes, allusions, or other literary devices to convey the theme. An author's use of diction, syntax, and tone can also help convey the theme. Authors will often develop themes through the development of characters, use of the setting, repetition of ideas, use of symbols, and through contrasting value systems. Authors of both fiction and nonfiction genres will use a variety of these techniques to develop one or more themes.

Regardless of the literary genre, there are commonalities in how authors, playwrights, and poets develop themes or central ideas.

Authors often do research, the results of which contributes to theme. In prose fiction and drama, this research may include real historical information about the setting the author has chosen or include elements that make fictional characters, settings, and plots seem realistic to the reader. In nonfiction, research is critical since the information contained within this literature must be accurate and, moreover, accurately represented.

In fiction, authors present a narrative conflict that will contribute to the overall theme. In fiction, this conflict may involve the storyline itself and some trouble between characters that needs resolution. In nonfiction, this conflict may be an explanation or commentary on factual people and events.

Authors will sometimes use character motivation to convey theme, such as in the example from *Hamlet* regarding revenge. In fiction, the characters will think, speak, and act in ways that effectively convey the theme to readers. In nonfiction, the characters are factual, as in a biography, but authors pay particular attention to presenting specific motivations to make the theme clear to readers.

Authors also use literary devices as a means of conveying theme. For example, the use of moon symbolism in Shelley's *Frankenstein* is significant as its phases can be compared to the phases that the Creature undergoes as he struggles with his identity.

The selected point of view can also contribute to a text's theme. The use of first-person point-of-view in a fiction or nonfiction work engages the reader's response differently than third-person point-of-view. The central idea or theme from a first-person narrative may differ from a third-person limited text.

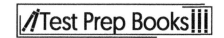

In literary nonfiction, authors usually identify the purpose of their writing, which differs from fiction where the general purpose is to entertain. The purpose of nonfiction is usually to inform, persuade, or entertain the audience. The stated purpose of a non-fiction text will drive how the central message or theme, if applicable, is presented.

Authors identify an audience for their writing, which is critical in shaping the theme of the work. For example, the audience for J.K. Rowling's *Harry Potter* series would be different than the audience for a biography of George Washington. The audience an author chooses to address is closely tied to the purpose of the work. The choice of an audience also drives the choice of language and level of diction an author uses. Ultimately, the intended audience determines the level to which that subject matter is presented and the complexity of the theme.

Author's Point of View and Writing Strategies

A **rhetorical strategy**—also referred to as a **rhetorical mode**—is the structural way an author chooses to present their argument. Though the terms noted below are similar to the organizational structures noted earlier, these strategies do not imply that the entire text follows the approach. For example, a cause and effect organizational structure is solely that, nothing more. A persuasive text may use cause and effect as a strategy to convey a singular point. Thus, an argument may include several of the strategies as the author strives to convince their audience to take action or accept a different point of view. It's important that readers are able to identify an author's thesis and position on the topic in order to be able to identify the careful construction through which the author speaks to the reader. The following are some of the more common rhetorical strategies:

- **Cause and effect**—establishing a logical correlation or causation between two ideas
- **Classification/division**—the grouping of similar items together or division of something into parts
- **Comparison/contrast**—the distinguishing of similarities/differences to expand on an idea
- **Definition**—used to clarify abstract ideas, unfamiliar concepts, or to distinguish one idea from another
- **Description**—use of vivid imagery, active verbs, and clear adjectives to explain ideas
- **Exemplification**—the use of examples to explain an idea
- **Narration**—anecdotes or personal experience to present or expand on a concept
- **Problem/Solution**—presentation of a problem or problems, followed by proposed solution(s)

Types of Passages

There are four main types of writing: narrative, expository, descriptive, and persuasive. Though these types are not mutually exclusive, one form tends to dominate the rest. By recognizing the type of passage you're reading, you gain insight into how you should read. If you're reading a narrative, you can assume the author intends to entertain, which means you may skim the text without losing meaning.

Narrative writing: When an author writes a narrative, they are telling a story. Narratives develop characters, drive a sequence of events, and deal with conflict. Examples of classic narratives are *The Great Gatsby*, *One Hundred Years of Solitude*, and *Song of Solomon*.

Expository writing: Expository writing is meant to instruct or inform and usually lacks any kind of persuasive elements. Expository writing includes recipes, academic lessons, repair manuals, or newspaper articles. Expository writing in academia uses third-person point of view and strives to be non-bias in its presentation.

Descriptive writing: Descriptive writing is writing that uses imagery and figurative language in order to allow the reader to feel as if they are experiencing the text firsthand. For example, a descriptive paragraph about Heather eating an ice cream cone will detail the smooth cream dripping down the cone, the crunch waffle, and the coldness and sweetness of the first bite. The reader is feeling the experience through the author's sensory language.

Persuasive writing: Persuasive writing is used when someone is writing an argument. Authors using persuasive writing are attempting to change the opinions and attitudes of their audience. Good persuasive writing will use credible sources and thoughtful analysis, stating both sides of the argument unbiasedly.

Fictional Prose

Fiction written in prose can be further broken down into **fiction genres**—types of fiction. Some of the more common genres of fiction are as follows:

- **Classical fiction**: a work of fiction considered timeless in its message or theme, remaining noteworthy and meaningful over decades or centuries—e.g., Charlotte Brontë's *Jane Eyre*, Mark Twain's *Adventures of Huckleberry Finn*

- **Fables**: short fiction that generally features animals, fantastic creatures, or other forces within nature that assume human-like characters and has a moral lesson for the reader—e.g., *Aesop's Fables*

- **Fairy tales**: children's stories with magical characters in imaginary, enchanted lands, usually depicting a struggle between good and evil, a sub-genre of folklore—e.g., Hans Christian Anderson's *The Little Mermaid*, *Cinderella* by the Brothers Grimm

- **Fantasy**: fiction with magic or supernatural elements that cannot occur in the real world, sometimes involving medieval elements in language, usually includes some form of sorcery or witchcraft and sometimes set on a different world—e.g., J.R.R. Tolkien's *The Hobbit*, J.K. Rowling's *Harry Potter and the Sorcerer's Stone*, George R.R. Martin's *A Game of Thrones*

- **Folklore**: types of fiction passed down from oral tradition, stories indigenous to a particular region or culture, with a local flavor in tone, designed to help humans cope with their condition in life and validate cultural traditions, beliefs, and customs—e.g., William Laughead's *Paul Bunyan and The Blue Ox*, the Buddhist story of "The Banyan Deer"

- **Mythology**: closely related to folklore but more widespread, features mystical, otherworldly characters and addresses the basic question of why and how humans exist, relies heavily on allegory and features gods or heroes captured in some sort of struggle—e.g., Greek myths, Genesis I and II in the Bible, Arthurian legends

- **Science fiction**: fiction that uses the principle of extrapolation—loosely defined as a form of prediction—to imagine future realities and problems of the human experience—e.g., Robert Heinlein's *Stranger in a Strange Land*, Ayn Rand's *Anthem*, Isaac Asimov's *I, Robot*, Philip K. Dick's *Do Androids Dream of Electric Sheep?*

- **Short stories**: short works of prose fiction with fully-developed themes and characters, focused on mood, generally developed with a single plot, with a short period of time for settings—e.g.,

Edgar Allan Poe's "Fall of the House of Usher," Shirley Jackson's "The Lottery," Isaac Bashevis Singer's "Gimpel the Fool"

Drama

Drama refers to a form of literature written for the purpose of performance for an audience. Like prose fiction, drama has several genres. The following are the most common ones:

- **Comedy**: a humorous play designed to amuse and entertain, often with an emphasis on the common person's experience, generally resolved in a positive way—e.g., Richard Sheridan's *School for Scandal*, Shakespeare's *Taming of the Shrew*, Neil Simon's *The Odd Couple*

- **History**: a play based on recorded history where the fate of a nation or kingdom is at the core of the conflict—e.g., Christopher Marlowe's *Edward II*, Shakespeare's *King Richard III*, Arthur Miller's *The Crucible*

- **Tragedy**: a serious play that often involves the downfall of the protagonist. In modern tragedies, the protagonist is not necessarily in a position of power or authority—e.g., Jean Racine's *Phèdre*, Arthur Miller's *Death of a Salesman*, John Steinbeck's *Of Mice and Men*

- **Melodrama**: a play that emphasizes heightened emotion and sensationalism, generally with stereotypical characters in exaggerated or realistic situations and with moral polarization—e.g., Jean-Jacques Rousseau's *Pygmalion*

- **Tragi-comedy**: a play that has elements of both tragedy—a character experiencing a tragic loss—and comedy—the resolution is often positive with no clear distinctive mood for either—e.g., Shakespeare's *The Merchant of Venice*, Anton Chekhov's *The Cherry Orchard*

Poetry

The genre of **poetry** refers to literary works that focus on the expression of feelings and ideas through the use of structure and linguistic rhythm to create a desired effect.

Different poetic structures and devices are used to create the various major forms of poetry. Some of the most common forms are discussed in the following chart.

Type	Poetic Structure	Example
Ballad	A poem or song passed down orally which tells a story and in English tradition usually uses an ABAB or ABCB rhyme scheme	William Butler Yeats' "The Ballad of Father O'Hart"
Epic	A long poem from ancient oral tradition which narrates the story of a legendary or heroic protagonist	Homer's *The Odyssey* Virgil's *The Aeneid*
Haiku	A Japanese poem of three unrhymed lines with five, seven, and five syllables (in English) with nature as a common subject matter	Matsuo Bashō "An old silent pond . . . A frog jumps into the pond, splash! Silence again."
Limerick	A five-line poem written in an AABBA rhyme scheme, with a witty focus	From Edward Lear's *Book of Nonsense*: "There was a Young Person of Smyrna Whose grandmother threatened to burn her . . ."
Ode	A formal lyric poem that addresses and praises a person, place, thing, or idea	Edna St. Vincent Millay's "Ode to Silence"
Sonnet	A fourteen-line poem written in iambic pentameter	Shakespeare's Sonnets 18 and 130

Metrical Feet

The most popular line used in poetry is called **iambic pentameter**. **Iambs** are a metrical foot consisting of unstressed then stressed syllables. Pentameter means there are five of those iambs in a single line. Count the stresses in the line below:

And summer's lease hath all too short a date.

The stresses go on the following words: "sum, lease, all, short, date." When spoken aloud, these syllables are all stressed in the sentence, which means we put more emphasis on them than the other syllables. We have five iambs (unstressed/stress) in this line, which makes it iambic pentameter. Let's say we had a line of iambic tetrameter. This is what many nursery rhymes are made of. Here is a line of iambic tetrameter:

The mouse sat down inside a cup.

The stresses go on the following words: "mouse, down, side, cup." If you count the number of times you stress a word, it's four times. Thus, the line is iambic tetrameter.

There are so many different kinds of metrical feet other than iambs. Here is a short list of metrical feet:

- Iamb: unstressed, stressed (2 syllables) ("aboard")
- Trochee: stressed, unstressed (2 syllables) ("apple")

- Dactylic: stressed, unstressed, unstressed (3 syllables) ("elephant")
- Anapest: unstressed, unstressed, stressed (3 syllables) ("contradict")

The following is a list of different lines of verse counts:

- Monometer: a line with one foot
- Dimeter: a line with two feet
- Trimeter: a line with three feet
- Tetrameter: a line with four feet
- Pentameter: a line with five feet
- Hexameter: a line with six feet
- Heptameter: a line with seven feet
- Octameter: a line with eight feet

The most popular line of verse in the English language is iambic pentameter, because it is the most natural sounding of all the verses. If someone is speaking in iambic pentameter, it will be extremely subtle. However, someone speaking in iambic tetrameter may sound like they are reciting a nursery rhyme.

Literary Nonfiction

Nonfiction works are best characterized by their subject matter, which must be factual and real, describing true life experiences. There are several common types of literary non-fiction.

Biography

A **biography** is a work written about a real person (historical or currently living). It involves factual accounts of the person's life, often in a re-telling of those events based on available, researched factual information. The re-telling and dialogue, especially if related within quotes, must be accurate and reflect reliable sources. A biography reflects the time and place in which the person lived, with the goal of creating an understanding of the person and their human experience. Examples of well-known biographies include *The Life of Samuel Johnson* by James Boswell and *Steve Jobs* by Walter Isaacson.

Autobiography

An **autobiography** is a factual account of a person's life written by that person. It may contain some or all of the same elements as a biography, but the author is the subject matter. An autobiography will be told in first person narrative. Examples of well-known autobiographies in literature include *Night* by Elie Wiesel and *Margaret Thatcher: The Autobiography* by Margaret Thatcher.

Memoir

A **memoir** is a historical account of a person's life and experiences written by one who has personal, intimate knowledge of the information. The line between memoir, autobiography, and biography is often muddled, but generally speaking, a memoir covers a specific timeline of events as opposed to the other forms of nonfiction. A memoir is less all-encompassing. It is also less formal in tone and tends to focus on the emotional aspect of the presented timeline of events. Some examples of memoirs in literature include *Angela's Ashes* by Frank McCourt and *All Creatures Great and Small* by James Herriot.

Journalism

Some forms of **journalism** can fall into the category of literary non-fiction—e.g., travel writing, nature writing, sports writing, the interview, and sometimes, the essay. Some examples include Elizabeth Kolbert's "The Lost World, in the Annals of Extinction series for *The New Yorker* and Gary Smith's "Ali and His Entourage" for *Sports Illustrated*.

Example Passage

Developing a knowledge of diverse texts other than those in western literature is an important part of learning about other cultures and their point of view. Since literature reflects the time period, consciousness, and perspectives of a culture, reading diverse texts in alternate time periods is a fundamental way to experience cultures other than our own. We might not only learn compassion but a well-rounded view of life and experiences around the world. The following list depicts world literature classics from other cultures, although the list is not comprehensive:

- *Don Quixote* by Miguel de Cervantes
- *Things Fall Apart* by Chinua Achebe
- *Pride and Prejudice* by Jane Austen
- *Wuthering Heights* by Emily Bronte
- *Heart of Darkness* by Joseph Conrad
- *The Stranger* by Albert Camus
- *The Divine Comedy* by Dante Alighieri
- *Canterbury Tales* by Geoffrey Chaucer
- *Great Expectations* by Charles Dickens
- *Madame Bovary* by Gustave Flaubert
- *One Hundred Years of Solitude* by Gabriel Garcia Marquez
- *The Iliad and The Odyssey* by Homer
- *The Trial* by Franz Kafka
- *The Sound of the Mountain* by Yasunari Kawabata
- *Diary of a Madman and Other Stories* by Lun Xun
- *The Tale of Genji* by Murasaki Shikibu
- *Lolita* by Vladimir Nabokov
- *The Book of Disquiet* by Fernando Pessoa
- *War and Peace* by Leo Tolstoy
- *Mrs. Dalloway* by Virginia Woolf
- *Nectar in a Sieve* by Kamala Markandaya
- *Obasan* by Joy Kogawa
- *The House of the Spirits* by Isabel Allende

Let's look at an example of a world literature classic and its surrounding context. The following is a passage from the narrative poem, The *Divine Comedy*, written by Dante Alighieri, an Italian poet in the late Middle ages.

Benign Apollo! this last labour aid,

And make me such a vessel of thy worth,

As thy own laurel claims of me belov'd.

Thus far hath one of steep Parnassus' brows

Suffic'd me; henceforth there is need of both

For my remaining enterprise Do thou

Enter into my bosom, and there breathe

So, as when Marsyas by thy hand was dragg'd

Forth from his limbs unsheath'd. O power divine!

If thou to me of shine impart so much,

That of that happy realm the shadow'd form

Trac'd in my thoughts I may set forth to view,

Thou shalt behold me of thy favour'd tree

Come to the foot, and crown myself with leaves;

For to that honour thou, and my high theme

Will fit me. If but seldom, might Sire!

To grace his triumph gathers thence a wreath

Caesar or bard (more shame for human wills

Deprav'd!) joy to the Delphic god must spring

From the Pierian foliage, when one breast

Is with such thirst inspir'd. From a small spark

Great flame hath risen; after me perchance

Others with better voice may pray, and gain

From the Cirrhaean city answer kind.

This text was written in the Middle Ages, as you can probably tell from the language using "thy" and "thou." Remember that most texts in world literature from other countries that you read in English are probably translated into English. This poem was originally written in Italian. The original poem in Italian has a different rhyme scheme and metrical line than the one above. The above is iambic pentameter, which is a popular line for a poet to use in English because it fits nicely with the way we stress our words. In the original Italian, the poem is written in terza rima, which is a rhyme scheme that fits well with the Italian language because many of the word-endings in Italian are easier to rhyme than in English.

In the poem above, the poet is calling on Apollo for inspiration, who is the god of poetry. This rhetorical device of calling out to an abstract thing is called an apostrophe and is used by many poets throughout the centuries, though this device is less common now. In epic poems or medieval narrative poems, it was very popular for the author to dedicate a passage to the gods before embarking on the journey, or narrative. Knowing characteristics and context of world literature can help us to understand cultures better in the past and why they did certain things.

Narration

Author's Purpose

No matter the genre or format, all authors are writing to persuade, inform, entertain, or express feelings. Often, these purposes are blended, with one dominating the rest. It's useful to learn to recognize the author's purpose.

Authors sometimes want to persuade or convince readers of something. This type of writing often contains two elements: the argument and the counterargument. The argument takes a stance on an issue, while the counterargument pokes holes in the opposition's stance. Authors rely on logic, emotion, and writer credibility to persuade readers to agree with them. If readers are opposed to the stance before reading, they are unlikely to adopt that stance. However, those who are undecided or committed to the same stance are more likely to agree with the author.

Sometimes authors want to teach or inform. Workplace manuals, instructor lessons, statistical reports and cookbooks are examples of informative texts. Informative writing is usually based on facts and is often void of emotion and persuasion. Informative texts generally contain statistics, charts, and graphs. Though most informative texts lack a persuasive agenda, readers must examine the text carefully to determine whether one exists within a given passage.

Sometimes authors want to entertain by writing stories or narratives. When you go to the movies, you often want to escape for a few hours, not necessarily to think critically. Entertaining writing is designed to delight and engage the reader. However, sometimes this type of writing can be woven into more serious materials, such as persuasive or informative writing to hook the reader before transitioning into a more scholarly discussion.

Sometimes authors want to draw an emotion out of the reader. This type of writing works to evoke the reader's feelings, such as anger, euphoria, or sadness. The connection between reader and author is an attempt to cause the reader to share the author's intended emotion or tone. Sometimes in order to make a piece more poignant, the author simply wants readers to feel emotion that the author has felt. Other times, the author attempts to persuade or manipulate the reader into adopting their stance. While it's okay to sympathize with the author, be aware of the individual's underlying intent.

Author's Style, Tone, and Mood

Style, tone, and mood are often thought to be the same thing. Though they're closely related, there are important differences to keep in mind. The easiest way to do this is to remember that style creates and affects tone and mood. More specifically, style is how the writer uses words to create the desired tone and mood for their writing.

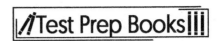

Style

Style can include any number of technical writing choices, and some may have to be analyzed on the test. A few examples of style choices include:

- **Sentence Construction**: When presenting facts, does the writer use shorter sentences to create a quicker sense of the supporting evidence, or do they use longer sentences to elaborate and explain the information?

- **Technical Language**: Does the writer use jargon to demonstrate their expertise in the subject, or do they use ordinary language to help the reader understand things in simple terms?

- **Formal Language**: Does the writer refrain from using contractions such as *won't* or *can't* to create a more formal tone, or do they use a colloquial, conversational style to connect to the reader?

- **Formatting**: Does the writer use a series of shorter paragraphs to help the reader follow a line of argument, or do they use longer paragraphs to examine an issue in great detail and demonstrate their knowledge of the topic?

On the test, examine the writer's style and how their writing choices affect the way the text comes across.

Tone

Tone refers to the writer's attitude toward the subject matter. For example, the tone conveys how the writer feels about the topic they are writing about. A lot of nonfiction writing has a neutral tone, which is an important tone for the writer to take. A neutral tone demonstrates that the writer is presenting a topic impartially and letting the information speak for itself. On the other hand, nonfiction writing can be just as effective and appropriate if the tone isn't neutral. For instance, consider this example:

Seat belts save more lives than any other automobile safety feature. Many studies show that airbags save lives as well; however, not all cars have airbags. For instance, some older cars don't. Furthermore, air bags aren't entirely reliable. For example, studies show that in 15% of accidents, airbags don't deploy as designed; but, on the other hand, seat belt malfunctions are extremely rare. The number of highway fatalities has plummeted since laws requiring seat belt usage were enacted.

In this passage, the writer mostly chooses to retain a neutral tone when presenting information. If the writer would instead include their own personal experience of losing a friend or family member in a car accident, the tone would change dramatically. The tone would no longer be neutral and would show that the writer has a personal stake in the content, allowing them to interpret the information in a different way. When analyzing tone, consider what the writer is trying to achieve in the text and how they *create* the tone using style.

Mood

Mood refers to the feelings and atmosphere that the writer's words create for the reader. Like tone, many nonfiction texts can have a neutral mood. To return to the previous example, if the writer chose to include information about a person they knew dying in a car accident, the text would carry an emotional component that is absent in the previous example. Depending on how they present the information, the writer can create a sad, angry, or even hopeful mood. When analyzing the mood, consider what the writer wants to accomplish and whether the best choice was made to achieve that end.

Fact and Opinion, Biases, and Stereotypes

It is important to distinguish between facts and opinions when reading a text. When an author presents **facts**, such as statistics or data, readers should be able to check those facts to verify that they are accurate. When authors share their own thoughts and feelings about a subject, they are expressing their **opinions**.

Authors often use words like *think, feel, believe,* or *in my opinion* when expressing an opinion, but these words won't always appear in an opinion piece, especially if it is formally written. An author's opinion may be backed up by facts, which gives it more credibility, but that opinion should not be taken as fact. A critical reader should be suspect of an author's opinion, especially if it is only supported by other opinions.

Fact	Opinion
There are nine innings in a game of baseball.	Baseball games run too long.
James Garfield was assassinated on July 2, 1881.	James Garfield was a good president.
McDonald's® has stores in 118 countries.	McDonald's® has the best hamburgers.

Critical readers examine the facts used to support an author's argument. They check the facts against other sources to be sure those facts are correct. They also check the validity of the sources used to be sure those sources are credible, academic, and/or peer-reviewed. When an author uses another person's opinion to support their argument, even if it is an expert's opinion, it is still only an opinion and should not be taken as fact. A strong argument uses valid, measurable facts to support ideas. Even then, the reader may disagree with the argument.

An authoritative argument may use the facts to sway the reader. In the example of global warming, many experts differ in their opinions of which alternative fuels can be used to aid in offsetting it. Because of this, a writer may choose to only use the information and expert opinions that support their viewpoint. For example, if the argument is that wind energy is the best solution, the author will use facts that support this idea. That same author may leave out relevant facts on solar energy. The way the author uses facts can influence the reader, so it's important to consider the facts being used, how those facts are being presented, and what information might be left out.

Authors can also demonstrate **bias** if they ignore an opposing viewpoint or present their side in an unbalanced way. A strong argument considers the opposition and finds a way to refute it. Critical readers should look for an unfair or one-sided presentation of the argument and be skeptical, as a bias may be present. Even if this bias is unintentional, if it exists in the writing, the reader should be wary of the validity of the argument.

Readers should also look for the use of stereotypes that refer to specific groups. **Stereotypes** are often negative connotations about a person or place and should always be avoided. When a critical reader finds stereotypes in a piece of writing, they should immediately be critical of the argument and consider the validity of anything the author presents. Stereotypes reveal a flaw in the writer's thinking and may suggest a lack of knowledge or understanding about the subject.

Figurative Language

Similes and **metaphors** are types of figurative language that are used as rhetorical devices. Both are comparisons between two things, but their formats differ slightly. A simile says that two things are similar and makes a comparison using "like" or "as"—*A* is like *B*, or *A* is as [some characteristic] as *B*— whereas a metaphor states that two things are exactly the same—*A* is *B*. In both cases, similes and metaphors invite the reader to think more deeply about the characteristics of the two subjects and consider where they overlap. Sometimes the poet develops a complex metaphor throughout the entire poem; this is known as an extended metaphor. An example of metaphor can be found in the sentence: "His pillow was a fluffy cloud." An example of simile can be found in the first line of Robert Burns' famous poem:

> My love is like a red, red rose

This is comparison using "like," and the two things being compared are love and a rose. Some characteristics of a rose are that it is fragrant, beautiful, blossoming, colorful, vibrant—by comparing his love to a red, red rose, Burns asks the reader to apply these qualities of a rose to his love. In this way, he implies that his love is also fresh, blossoming, and brilliant.

In addition to rhetorical devices that play on the meanings of words, there are also rhetorical devices that use the sounds of words. These devices are most often found in poetry but may also be found in other types of literature and in nonfiction writing like texts for speeches.

Alliteration and assonance are both varieties of sound repetition. Other types of sound repetition include: **anaphora**—repetition that occurs at the beginning of the sentences; **epiphora**—repetition occurring at the end of phrases; **antimetabole**—repetition of words in a succession; and **antiphrasis**—a form of denial of an assertion in a text.

Alliteration refers to the repetition of the first sound of each word. Recall Robert Burns' opening line:

> My love is like a red, red rose

This line includes two instances of alliteration: "love" and "like" (repeated *L* sound), as well as "red" and "rose" (repeated *R* sound). Next, **assonance** refers to the repetition of vowel sounds, and can occur anywhere within a word (not just the opening sound). Here is the opening of a poem by John Keats:

> When I have fears that I may cease to be
>
> Before my pen has glean'd my teeming brain

Assonance can be found in the words "fears," "cease," "be," "glean'd," and "teeming," all of which stress the long *E* sound. Both alliteration and assonance create a harmony that unifies the writer's language.

Another sound device is **onomatopoeia**—words whose spelling mimics the sound they describe. Words like "crash," "bang," and "sizzle" are all examples of onomatopoeia. Use of onomatopoetic language adds auditory imagery to the text.

Readers are probably most familiar with the technique of using a **pun**. A pun is a play on words, taking advantage of two words that have the same or similar pronunciation. Puns can be found throughout Shakespeare's plays, for instance:

> Now is the winter of our discontent
>
> Made glorious summer by this son of York

These lines from *Richard III* contain a play on words. Richard III refers to his brother—the newly crowned King Edward IV—as the "son of York," referencing their family heritage from the house of York. However, while drawing a comparison between the political climate and the weather (times of political trouble were the "winter," but now the new king brings "glorious summer"), Richard's use of the word "son" also implies another word with the same pronunciation, "sun"—so Edward IV is also like the sun, bringing light, warmth, and hope to England. Puns are a clever way for writers to suggest two meanings at once.

Figures of speech may sometimes use one word in place of another. **Synecdoche**, for example, uses a part of something to refer to its whole. The expression "Don't hurt a hair on her head!" implies protecting more than just an individual hair, but rather her entire body. "The art teacher is training a class of Picassos" uses Picasso, one individual notable artist, to stand in for the entire category of talented artists. Another figure of speech using word replacement is **metonymy**, where a word is replaced with something closely associated to it. For example, news reports may use the word "Washington" to refer to the American government or "the crown" to refer to the British monarch.

Below is a list of figurative language with their definitions and examples:

Device	Definition	Example
Alliteration	Repeating the same beginning sound or letter in a phrase for emphasis	The busy baby babbled.
Allusion	A reference to a famous person, event, or significant literary text as a form of significant comparison	"We are apt to shut our eyes against a painful truth, and listen to the song of that siren till she transforms us into beasts." Patrick Henry
Anaphora	The repetition of the same words at the beginning of successive words, phrases, or clauses, designed to emphasize an idea	"We shall not flag or fail. We shall go on to the end. We shall fight in France, we shall fight on the seas and oceans, we shall fight with growing confidence … we shall fight in the fields and in the streets, we shall fight in the hills. We shall never surrender." Winston Churchill
Antithesis	A part of speech where a contrast of ideas is expressed by a pair of words that are opposite of each other.	"That's one small step for man, one giant leap for mankind." Neil Armstrong
Foreshadowing	Giving an indication that something is going to happen later in the story	I wasn't aware at the time, but I would come to regret those words.
Hyperbole	Using exaggeration not meant to be taken literally	The girl weighed less than a feather.
Idiom	Using words with predictable meanings to create a phrase with a different meaning	The world is your oyster.
Imagery	Appealing to the senses by using descriptive language	The sky was painted with red and pink and streaked with orange.
Metaphor	Compares two things as if they are the same	He was a giant teddy bear.
Onomatopoeia	Using words that imitate sound	The tire went off with a bang and a crunch.
Parallelism	A syntactical similarity in a structure or series of structures used for impact of an idea, making it memorable	"A penny saved is a penny earned." Ben Franklin
Personification	Attributing human characteristics to an object or an animal	The house glowered menacingly with a dark smile.

Device	Definition	Example
Rhetorical question	A question posed that is not answered by the writer though there is a desired response, most often designed to emphasize a point	"Can anyone look at our reduced standing in the world today and say, 'Let's have four more years of this?'" Ronald Reagan
Simile	Compares two things using "like" or "as"	Her hair was like gold.
Symbolism	Using symbols to represent ideas and provide a different meaning	The ring represented the bond between us.
Understatement	A statement meant to portray a situation as less important than it actually is to create an ironic effect	"The war in the Pacific has not necessarily developed in Japan's favor." Emperor Hirohito, surrendering Japan in World War II

Sarcasm

Depending on the tone of voice or the words used, sarcasm can be expressed in many different ways. **Sarcasm** is defined as a bitter or ambiguous declaration that intends to cut or taunt. Most of the ways we use sarcasm is saying something and not really meaning it. In a way, sarcasm is a contradiction that is understood by both the speaker and the listener to convey the opposite meaning. For example, let's say Bobby is struggling to learn how to play the trumpet. His sister, Gloria, walks in and tells him: "What a great trumpet player you've become!" This is a sort of verbal irony known as sarcasm. Gloria is speaking a contradiction, but Bobby and Gloria both know the truth behind what she's saying: that Bobby is not a good trumpet player. Sarcasm can also be accompanied by nonverbal language, such as a smirk or a head tilt. Remember that sarcasm is not always clear to the listener; sometimes sarcasm can be expressed by the speaker but lost on the listener.

Irony

Irony is a device that authors use when pitting two contrasting items or ideas against each other in order to create an effect. It's frequently used when an author wants to employ humor or convey a sarcastic tone. Additionally, it's often used in fictional works to build tension between characters, or between a particular character and the reader. An author may use **verbal irony** (sarcasm), **situational irony** (where actions or events have the opposite effect than what's expected), and **dramatic irony** (where the reader knows something a character does not). Examples of irony include:

- Dramatic Irony: An author describing the presence of a hidden killer in a murder mystery, unbeknownst to the characters but known to the reader.

- Situational Irony: An author relating the tale of a fire captain who loses her home in a five-alarm conflagration.

- Verbal Irony: This is where an author or character says one thing but means another. For example, telling a police officer "Thanks a lot" after receiving a ticket.

Understatement

Making an **understatement** means making a statement that gives the illusion of something being smaller than it actually is. Understatement is used, in some instances, as a humorous rhetorical device. Let's say that there are two friends. One of the friends, Kate, meets the other friend's, Jasmine's, boyfriend. Jasmine's boyfriend, in Kate's opinion, is attractive, funny, and intelligent. After Kate meets her friend's boyfriend, Kate says to Jasmine, "You could do worse." Kate and Jasmine both know from Kate's tone that this means Kate is being ironic—Jasmine could do much, much worse, because her boyfriend is considered a "good catch." The understatement was a rhetorical device used by Kate to let Jasmine know she approves.

Directly Stated Information vs. Implications

Engaged readers should constantly self-question while reviewing texts to help them form conclusions. Self-questioning is when readers review a paragraph, page, passage, or chapter and ask themselves, "Did I understand what I read?," "What was the main event in this section?," "Where is this taking place?," and so on. Authors can provide clues or pieces of evidence throughout a text or passage to guide readers toward a conclusion. This is why active and engaged readers should read the text or passage in its entirety before forming a definitive conclusion. If readers do not gather all the pieces of evidence needed, then they may jump to an illogical conclusion.

At times, authors directly state conclusions while others simply imply them. Of course, it is easier if authors outwardly provide conclusions to readers because it does not leave any information open to interpretation. On the other hand, implications are things that authors do not directly state but can be assumed based off of information they provided. If authors only imply what may have happened, readers can form a menagerie of ideas for conclusions. For example, look at the following statement: "Once we heard the sirens, we hunkered down in the storm shelter." In this statement, the author does not directly state that there was a tornado, but clues such as "sirens" and "storm shelter" provide insight to the readers to help form that conclusion.

Connotation and Denotation

Connotation is when an author chooses words or phrases that invoke ideas or feelings other than their literal meaning. An example of the use of connotation is the word *cheap*, which suggests something is poor in value or negatively describes a person as reluctant to spend money. When something or someone is described this way, the reader is more inclined to have a particular image or feeling about it or him/her. Thus, connotation can be a very effective language tool in creating emotion and swaying opinion. However, connotations are sometimes hard to pin down because varying emotions can be associated with a word. Generally, though, connotative meanings tend to be fairly consistent within a specific cultural group.

Denotation refers to words or phrases that mean exactly what they say. It is helpful when a writer wants to present hard facts or vocabulary terms with which readers may be unfamiliar. Some examples of denotation are the words *inexpensive* and *frugal*. *Inexpensive* refers to the cost of something, not its value, and *frugal* indicates that a person is conscientiously watching his or her spending. These terms do not elicit the same emotions that *cheap* does.

Authors sometimes choose to use both, but what they choose and when they use it is what critical readers need to differentiate. One method isn't inherently better than the other; however, one may create a better effect, depending upon an author's intent. If, for example, an author's purpose is to inform, to instruct, and to familiarize readers with a difficult subject, their use of connotation may be helpful. However, it may also undermine credibility and confuse readers. An author who wants to create a credible, scholarly effect in a text would most likely use denotation, which emphasizes literal, factual meaning and examples.

Technical Language

Test takers and critical readers alike should be very aware of technical language used within informational text. **Technical language** refers to terminology that is specific to a particular industry and is best understood by those specializing in that industry. This language is fairly easy to differentiate, since it will most likely be unfamiliar to readers. It's critical to be able to define technical language either by the author's written definition, through the use of an included glossary—if offered—or through context clues that help readers clarify word meaning.

Analyzing an Author's Rhetorical Choices

Authors utilize a wide range of techniques to tell a story or communicate information. Readers should be familiar with the most common of these techniques. Techniques of writing are also known as **rhetorical devices**.

In nonfiction writing, authors employ argumentative techniques to present their opinions to readers in the most convincing way. Persuasive writing usually includes at least one type of **appeal**: an appeal to logic (**logos**), emotion (**pathos**), or credibility and trustworthiness (**ethos**). When writers appeal to logic, they are asking readers to agree with them based on research, evidence, and an established line of reasoning. An author's argument might also appeal to readers' emotions, perhaps by including personal stories and **anecdotes** (a short narrative of a specific event). A final type of appeal—appeal to authority—asks the reader to agree with the author's argument on the basis of their expertise or credentials. Three different approaches to arguing the same opinion are exemplified below:

Logic (Logos)

> Our school should abolish its current ban on cell phone use on campus. This rule was adopted last year as an attempt to reduce class disruptions and help students focus more on their lessons. However, since the rule was enacted, there has been no change in the number of disciplinary problems in class. Therefore, the rule is ineffective and should be done away with.

The above is an example of an appeal to logic. The author uses evidence to disprove the logic of the school's rule (the rule was supposed to reduce discipline problems, but the number of problems has not been reduced; therefore, the rule is not working) and to call for its repeal.

Emotion (Pathos)

An author's argument might also appeal to readers' emotions, perhaps by including personal stories and anecdotes.

The next example presents an appeal to emotion. By sharing the personal anecdote of one student and speaking about emotional topics like family relationships, the author invokes the reader's empathy in asking them to reconsider the school rule.

> Our school should abolish its current ban on cell phone use on campus. If they aren't able to use their phones during the school day, many students feel isolated from their loved ones. For example, last semester, one student's grandmother had a heart attack in the morning. However, because he couldn't use his cell phone, the student didn't

know about his grandmother's accident until the end of the day—when she had already passed away, and it was too late to say goodbye. By preventing students from contacting their friends and family, our school is placing undue stress and anxiety on students.

Credibility (Ethos)

Finally, an appeal to authority includes a statement from a relevant expert. In this case, the author uses a doctor in the field of education to support the argument. All three examples begin from the same opinion—the school's phone ban needs to change—but rely on different argumentative styles to persuade the reader.

> Our school should abolish its current ban on cell phone use on campus. According to Dr. Bartholomew Everett, a leading educational expert, "Research studies show that cell phone usage has no real impact on student attentiveness. Rather, phones provide a valuable technological resource for learning. Schools need to learn how to integrate this new technology into their curriculum." Rather than banning phones altogether, our school should follow the advice of experts and allow students to use phones as part of their learning.

Literary Argumentation

Understanding Authors' Claims

The goal of most persuasive and informative texts is to make a claim and support it with evidence. A **claim** is a statement made as though it is fact. Many claims are opinions; for example, "stealing is wrong." While this is generally true, it is arguable, meaning it is capable of being challenged. An initial reaction to "stealing is wrong" might be to agree; however, there may be circumstances in which it is warranted. If it is necessary for the survival of an individual or their loved ones (i.e., if they are starving and cannot afford to eat), then this assertion becomes morally ambiguous. While it may still be illegal, whether it is "wrong" is unclear.

When an assertion is made within a text, it is typically reinforced with supporting details as is exemplified in the following passage:

> The extinction of the dinosaurs has been a hot debate amongst scientists since the discovery of fossils in the eighteenth century. Numerous theories were developed in explanation, including extreme climate change, an epidemic of disease, or changes in the atmosphere. It wasn't until the late 1970s that a young geochemist, named Walter Alvarez, noticed significant changes in the soil layers of limestone he was studying in Italy. The layers contained fossilized remains of millions of small organisms within the layer that corresponded with the same period in which the dinosaurs lived. He noticed that the soil layer directly above this layer was suddenly devoid of any trace of these organisms. The soil layer directly above *this* layer was filled with an entirely new species of organisms. It seemed the first species had disappeared at the exact same time as the dinosaurs!
>
> With the help of his father, Walter Alvarez analyzed the soil layer between the extinct species and the new species and realized this layer was filled with an abnormal amount of *iridium* – a substance that is abundant in meteorites but almost never found on Earth. Unlike other elements in the fossil record, which take a long time to deposit, the iridium

had been laid down very abruptly. The layer also contained high levels of soot, enough to account for all of the earth's forests burning to the ground at the same time. This led scientists to create the best-supported theory that the tiny organisms, as well as the dinosaurs and countless other species, had been destroyed by a giant asteroid that had slammed into Earth, raining tons of iridium down on the planet from a giant cosmic cloud.

Supporting Claims

Before embarking on answering these questions, readers should summarize each. This will help in locating the supporting evidence. These summaries can be written down or completed mentally; full sentences are not necessary.

Paragraph 1: Layer of limestone shows that a species of organisms disappeared at same time as the dinosaurs

Paragraph 2: Layer had high amounts of iridium and soot – scientists believe dinosaurs destroyed by asteroid.

Simply by summarizing the text, it has been plainly outlined where there will be answers to relevant questions. Although there are often claims already embedded within an educational text, a claim will most likely be given, but the evidence to support it will need to be located. Take this example question:

> Q: What evidence within the text best supports the theory that the dinosaurs became extinct because of an asteroid?

The claim here is that the dinosaurs went extinct because of an asteroid. Because the text is already outlined in the summaries, it is easy to see that the evidence supporting this theory is in the second paragraph:

> With the help of his father, they analyzed the soil layer between the extinct species and the new species and realized this layer was filled with an abnormal amount of *iridium* – a substance that is abundant is meteorites but almost never found on Earth. Unlike other elements in the fossil record, which takes a long time to deposit, the iridium had been laid down very abruptly. The layer also contained high levels of soot, enough to account for all of the earth's forests burning to the ground at the same time. This led scientists to create the best-supported theory that the tiny organisms, as well as the dinosaurs and countless other species, had been destroyed by a giant asteroid that had slammed into Earth, raining tons of iridium down on the planet from a giant cosmic cloud.

Now that the evidence within the text that best supports the theory has been located, the answer choices can be evaluated:
  a. Changes in climate and atmosphere caused an asteroid to crash into Earth
  b. Walter and Luis Alvarez studied limestone with fossilized organisms
  c. A soil layer lacking organisms that existed at the same time as the dinosaurs showed low levels of iridium
  d. A soil layer lacking organisms that existed at the same time as the dinosaurs showed high levels of iridium

Answer choice (a) is clearly false as there is nothing within the text that claims that climate changes caused an asteroid to crash into Earth. This kind of answer choice displays an incorrect use of detail. Although the passage may have contained the words "change," "climate," and "atmosphere," these terms were manipulated to form an erroneous answer.

Answer choice (b) is incorrect because while the scientists did study limestone with fossilized organisms, and in doing so they discovered evidence that led to the formation of the theory, this is not the actual evidence itself. This is an example of an out-of-scope answer choice: a true statement that may or may not have been in the passage, but that isn't the whole answer or isn't the point.

Answer choice (c) is incorrect because it is the opposite of the correct answer. Assuming the second paragraph was summarized correctly, it is already known that the soil layer contained *high* levels of iridium, not low levels. Even if the paragraph was not summarized that way, the final sentence states that "tons of iridium rained down on the planet." So, answer choice (c) is false.

Answer choice (d) is correct because it matches the evidence found in the second paragraph.

Constructing Arguments Through Evidence

Using only one form of supporting evidence is not nearly as effective as using a variety to support a claim. Presenting only a list of statistics can be boring to the reader but providing a true story that's both interesting and humanizing helps. In addition, one example isn't always enough to prove the writer's larger point, so combining it with other examples in the writing is extremely effective. Thus, when reading a passage, readers should not just look for a single form of supporting evidence.

For example, although most people can't argue with the statement, "Seat belts save lives", its impact on the reader is much greater when supported by additional content. The writer can support this idea by:

- Providing statistics on the rate of highway fatalities alongside statistics of estimated seat belt usage.

- Explaining the science behind car accidents and what happens to a passenger who doesn't use a seat belt.

- Offering anecdotal evidence or true stories from reliable sources on how seat belts prevent fatal injuries in car crashes.

Another key aspect of supporting evidence is a **reliable source**. Does the writer include the source of the information? If so, is the source well-known and trustworthy? Is there a potential for bias? For example, a seat belt study done by a seat belt manufacturer may have its own agenda to promote.

Determining Whether a Statement Is or Is Not Supported

The basic tenet of reading comprehension is the ability to read and understand text. One way to understand text is to look for information that supports the author's main idea, topic, or position statement. This information may be factual, or it may be based on the author's opinion. This section will focus on the test taker's ability to identify factual information, as opposed to opinionated bias. The ACT will ask test takers to read passages containing factual information, and then logically relate those passages by drawing conclusions based on evidence.

In order to identify factual information within one or more text passages, begin by looking for statements of fact. Factual statements can be either true or false. Identifying factual statements as opposed to opinion statements is important in demonstrating full command of evidence in reading. For example, the statement *The temperature outside was unbearably hot* may seem like a fact; however, it's not. While anyone can point to a temperature gauge as factual evidence, the statement itself reflects only an opinion. Some people may find the temperature unbearably hot. Others may find it comfortably warm. Thus, the sentence, *The temperature outside was unbearably hot,* reflects the opinion of the author who found it unbearable. If the text passage followed up the sentence with atmospheric conditions indicating heat indices above 140 degrees Fahrenheit, then the reader knows there is factual information that supports the author's assertion of *unbearably hot.*

In looking for information that can be proven or disproven, it's helpful to scan for dates, numbers, timelines, equations, statistics, and other similar data within any given text passage. These types of indicators will point to proven particulars. For example, the statement, *The temperature outside was unbearably hot on that summer day, July 10, 1913,* most likely indicates factual information, even if the reader is unaware that this is the hottest day on record in the United States. Be careful when reading biased words from an author. Biased words indicate opinion, as opposed to fact. See the list of biased words below and keep in mind that it's not an inclusive list:

- Good/bad
- Great/greatest
- Better/best/worst
- Amazing
- Terrible/bad/awful
- Beautiful/handsome/ugly
- More/most
- Exciting/dull/boring
- Favorite
- Very
- Probably/should/seem/possibly

Remember, most of what is written is actually opinion or carefully worded information that seems like fact when it isn't. To say, *duplicating DNA results is not cost-effective* sounds like it could be a scientific fact, but it isn't. Factual information can be verified through independent sources.

The simplest type of test question may provide a text passage, then ask the test taker to distinguish the correct factual supporting statement that best answers the corresponding question on the test. However, be aware that most questions may ask the test taker to read more than one text passage and identify which answer best supports an author's topic. While the ability to identify factual information is critical, these types of questions require the test taker to identify chunks of details, and then relate them to one another.

Practice Questions

Questions 1–11 are based on the following passage:

"Mademoiselle Eugénie is pretty—I think I remember that to be her name."

"Very pretty, or rather, very beautiful," replied Albert, "but of that style of beauty which I don't appreciate; I am an ungrateful fellow."

"Really," said Monte Cristo, lowering his voice, "you don't appear to me to be very enthusiastic on the subject of this marriage."

"Mademoiselle Danglars is too rich for me," replied Morcerf, "and that frightens me."

"Bah," exclaimed Monte Cristo, "that's a fine reason to give. Are you not rich yourself?"

"My father's income is about 50,000 francs per annum; and he will give me, perhaps, ten or twelve thousand when I marry."

"That, perhaps, might not be considered a large sum, in Paris especially," said the count; "but everything doesn't depend on wealth, and it's a fine thing to have a good name, and to occupy a high station in society. Your name is celebrated, your position magnificent; and then the Comte de Morcerf is a soldier, and it's pleasing to see the integrity of a Bayard united to the poverty of a Duguesclin; disinterestedness is the brightest ray in which a noble sword can shine. As for me, I consider the union with Mademoiselle Danglars a most suitable one; she will enrich you, and you will ennoble her."

Albert shook his head and looked thoughtful. "There is still something else," said he.

"I confess," observed Monte Cristo, "that I have some difficulty in comprehending your objection to a young lady who is both rich and beautiful."

"Oh," said Morcerf, "this repugnance, if repugnance it may be called, isn't all on my side."

"Whence can it arise, then? for you told me your father desired the marriage."

"It's my mother who dissents; she has a clear and penetrating judgment and doesn't smile on the proposed union. I cannot account for it, but she seems to entertain some prejudice against the Danglars."

"Ah," said the count, in a somewhat forced tone, "that may be easily explained; the Comtesse de Morcerf, who is aristocracy and refinement itself, doesn't relish the idea of being allied by your marriage with one of ignoble birth; that is natural enough."

Excerpt from The Count of Monte Cristo, by Alexandre Dumas, 1844

1. The meaning of the word "repugnance" is closest to:
   a. Strong resemblance
   b. Strong dislike
   c. Extreme shyness
   d. Extreme dissimilarity

e. Intense suffering

2. What can be inferred about Albert's family?
    a. Their finances are uncertain.
    b. Albert is the only son in his family.
    c. Their name is more respected than the Danglars'.
    d. Albert's mother and father both agree on their decisions.
    e. No one wants Albert to be married at all.

3. What is Albert's attitude towards his impending marriage?
    a. Pragmatic
    b. Romantic
    c. Indifferent
    d. Apprehensive
    e. Animosity

4. What is the best description of the Count's relationship with Albert?
    a. He's like a strict parent, criticizing Albert's choices.
    b. He's like a wise uncle, giving practical advice to Albert.
    c. He's like a close friend, supporting all of Albert's opinions.
    d. He's like a suspicious investigator, asking many probing questions.
    e. He's like a stranger, listening politely but offering no advice.

5. Which sentence is true of Albert's mother?
    a. She belongs to a noble family.
    b. She often makes poor choices.
    c. She is primarily occupied with money.
    d. She is unconcerned about her son's future.
    e. She is supportive of the upcoming marriage.

6. Based on this passage, what is probably NOT true about French society in the 1800s?
    a. Children often received money from their parents.
    b. Marriages were sometimes arranged between families.
    c. Marriages were expected to be economically or socially beneficial to family.
    d. People were often expected to marry within their same social class.
    e. The richest people in society were also the most respected.

7. Why is the Count puzzled by Albert's attitude toward his marriage?
    a. He seems reluctant to marry Eugénie, despite her wealth and beauty.
    b. He is marrying against his father's wishes, despite usually following his advice.
    c. He appears excited to marry someone he doesn't love, despite being a hopeless romantic.
    d. He expresses reverence towards Eugénie, despite being from a higher social class than her.
    e. Albert knows the Count loved Eugénie first, yet he is still marrying her.

8. The passage is made up mostly of what kind of text?
    a. Narration
    b. Dialogue
    c. Description
    d. Explanation
    e. Information

9. What does the word "ennoble" mean in the middle of the passage?
   a. to create beauty in another person
   b. to endow someone with wealth
   c. to make someone chaste again
   d. to give someone a noble rank or title
   e. to provide someone with great joy

10. Why is the count said to have a "forced tone" in the last paragraph?
    a. Because he is in love with Mademoiselle Eugénie and is trying to keep it a secret.
    b. Because he finally agrees with Albert's point of view but still doesn't understand it.
    c. Because he finally understands Albert's point of view but still doesn't agree with it.
    d. Because he is only pretending that Albert is his friend to get information out of him.
    e. Because he is annoyed that Albert is getting married instead of himself.

11. Which of the following is true about Albert's father?
    a. He is a thief.
    b. He is a peasant.
    c. He is a king.
    d. He is a gangster.
    e. He is a soldier.

Answer Explanations

1. B: Strong dislike. This vocabulary question can be answered using context clues. Based on the rest of the conversation, the reader can gather that Albert isn't looking forward to his marriage. As the Count notes that "you don't appear to me to be very enthusiastic on the subject of this marriage," and also remarks on Albert's "objection to a young lady who is both rich and beautiful," readers can guess Albert's feelings. The answer choice that most closely matches "objection" and "not . . . very enthusiastic" is *B*, "strong dislike."

2. C: Their name is more respected than the Danglars'. This inference question can be answered by eliminating incorrect answers. Choice *A* is tempting, considering that Albert mentions money as a concern in his marriage. However, although he may not be as rich as his fiancée, his father still has a stable income of 50,000 francs a year. Choice *B* isn't mentioned at all in the passage, so it's impossible to make an inference. Choices *D* and *E* are both false because Albert's father arranged his marriage but his mother doesn't approve of it. Evidence for Choice *C* can be found in the Count's comparison of Albert and Eugénie: "she will enrich you, and you will ennoble her." In other words, the Danglars are wealthier, but the Morcerf family has a nobler background.

3. D: Apprehensive. There are many clues in the passage that indicate Albert's attitude towards his marriage—far from enthusiastic, he has many reservations. This question requires test takers to understand the vocabulary in the answer choices. "Pragmatic" is closest in meaning to "realistic," and "indifferent" means "uninterested." The word "animosity" is a bit strong, meaning extreme anger. The only word related to feeling worried, uncertain, or unfavorable about the future is "apprehensive."

4. B: He is like a wise uncle, giving practical advice to Albert. Choice *A* is incorrect because the Count's tone is friendly and conversational. Choice *C* is also incorrect because the Count questions why Albert doesn't want to marry a young, beautiful, and rich girl. While the Count asks many questions, he isn't particularly "probing" or "suspicious"—instead, he's asking to find out more about Albert's situation and then give him advice about marriage. The two men are not strangers, as the count does offer Albert some advice on his marriage.

5. A: She belongs to a noble family. Though Albert's mother doesn't appear in the scene, there's more than enough information to answer this question. More than once is his family's noble background mentioned (not to mention that Albert's mother is the Comtess de Morcerf, a noble title). The other answer choices can be eliminated—she is deeply concerned about her son's future; money isn't her highest priority because otherwise she would favor a marriage with the wealthy Danglars; she is not supportive of her son's marriage; and Albert describes her "clear and penetrating judgment," meaning she makes good decisions.

6. E: The richest people in society were also the most respected. The Danglars family is wealthier, but the Morcerf family has a more aristocratic name, which gives them a higher social standing. Evidence for the other answer choices can be found throughout the passage: Albert mentioned receiving money from his father's fortune after his marriage; Albert's father has arranged this marriage for him; and the Count speculates that Albert's mother disapproves of this marriage because Eugénie isn't from a noble background like the Morcerf family, implying that she would prefer a match with a girl from aristocratic society.

7. A: He seems reluctant to marry Eugénie, despite her wealth and beauty. This is a reading comprehension question, and the answer can be found in the following lines: "'I confess," observed Monte Cristo, "that I have some difficulty in comprehending your objection to a young lady who is both rich and beautiful."' Choice *B* is the opposite—Albert's father is the one who insists on the marriage. Choice *C* incorrectly represents Albert's eagerness to marry. Choice *D* describes a more positive attitude than Albert actually feels ("repugnance"). Choice *E* is not talked about in this passage.

8. B: The passage is mostly made up of dialogue. We can see this in the way the two characters communicate with each other, in this case through the use of quotations marks, or dialogue. Narration is when the narrator (not the characters) is explaining things that are happening in the story. Description is when the narrator describes a specific setting and its images. Explanation is when the author is analyzing or defining something for the reader's benefit. Informational text is when the author is simply presenting information to an audience.

9. D: The meaning of the word "ennoble" in the middle of the paragraph means to give someone a noble rank or title. In the passage, we can infer that Albert is noble but not rich, and Mademoiselle Eugénie is rich but not noble.

10. C: Because he finally understands Albert's point of view but still doesn't agree with it. The other choices aren't mentioned anywhere in the passage. Remember, although this passage is part of a larger text, the test taker should only pay attention to what's in the passage itself in order to find the correct answer.

11. E: Albert's father, the Comte de Morcerf, is a soldier. This information is provided in the middle longest paragraph, starting with the line, "'That, perhaps, might not be considered a large sum, in Paris especially,' said the count."

Composition

Analyzing an Essay

Aristotelian Rhetorical Analysis

Also known as the **Five Rhetorical Canons**, Aristotelian rhetorical analysis takes into consideration the various methods used to effectively persuade an audience using an oral platform. Aristotle, the great philosopher and rhetorician, lived in a time where most persuasion was done out loud in front of an audience. He used these canons as a guideline to effective speech and how to eloquently draw in an audience. Let's look at the five canons below:

- **Invention**: Invention can be seen as the first step in creating effective rhetoric. The speaker's relationship with the audience is important to this step, as the speaker uses this connection to invent the best possible way to reach their audience. Additionally, speakers should contemplate what the best possible medium is for their particular audience. Does the audience want a story? Would they be better receptive to a more ironical work, like a satire? Or would they want something serious and straightforward, like a description or analysis? Invention is how the speaker shapes their message in relation to an audience.

- **Arrangement**: The arrangement of a text is how the speaker chooses to organize the information presented. What should come first, and how should the rest of the text logically follow? Thinking about the audience is extremely important to arrangement, especially their position on the issue. A speaker would not want to approach a hostile audience by stating the opposite viewpoint straight away; the speaker would subtly and thoughtfully lead the audience to come to their own conclusion on an issue after all of the facts and rhetorical appeals are presented.

- **Style**: The style of a text is where the speaker's creative expression comes in. Or, as in technical or instructional writing, creative expression might be stifled for clarity's sake. The style of writing is the speaker/writer's lack or presence of creative expression and personality. Different ways to use style in speaking include tone, diction, figurative language, and word choice.

- **Memory**: Memory in rhetoric refers to the speaker being able to *recall* certain forms of memory or knowledge about their topic in case the audience has questions or asks the speaker to explain more on the subject. Memory is about the speaker's credibility and prior knowledge. Memory can also be about the speaker's knowledge of the audience and what *their* memory might entail, such as their own prior knowledge and assumptions they might have about the issue.

- **Delivery**: Delivery speaks to the credibility of the speaker or writer through *how* they deliver their message. Do they use proper syntax and punctuation? What is their timing like? Do they open with a proper introduction and end with a memorable conclusion? Does the delivery in the speech or writing involve excitement and passion, or is it critical and dull? Delivery is important to a speaker/author's credibility because good delivery relies on assessment of placement and timing.

Making Generalizations Based on Evidence

One way to make generalizations is to look for main topics. When doing so, pay particular attention to any titles, headlines, or opening statements made by the author. Topic sentences or repetitive ideas can be clues in gleaning inferred ideas. For example, if a passage contains the phrase *While some consider DNA testing to be infallible, it is an inherently flawed technique,* the test taker can infer the rest of the passage will contain information that points to problems with DNA testing.

The test taker may be asked to make a generalization based on prior knowledge but may also be asked to make predictions based on new ideas. For example, the test taker may have no prior knowledge of DNA other than its genetic property to replicate. However, if the reader is given passages on the flaws of DNA testing with enough factual evidence, the test taker may arrive at the inferred conclusion or generalization that the author does not support the infallibility of DNA testing in all identification cases.

When making generalizations, it is important to remember that the critical thinking process involved must be fluid and open to change. While a reader may infer an idea from a main topic, general statement, or other clues, they must be open to receiving new information within a particular passage. New ideas presented by an author may require the test taker to alter a generalization. Similarly, when asked questions that require making an inference, it's important to read the entire test passage and all of the answer options. Often, a test taker will need to refine a generalization based on new ideas that may be presented within the text itself.

Textual evidence within the details helps readers draw a conclusion about a passage. **Textual evidence** refers to information—facts and examples that support the main point. Textual evidence will likely come from outside sources and can be in the form of quoted or paraphrased material. In order to draw a conclusion from evidence, it's important to examine the credibility and validity of that evidence as well as how (and if) it relates to the main idea.

If an author presents a differing opinion or a **counterargument** in order to refute it, the reader should consider how and why this information is being presented. It is meant to strengthen the original argument and shouldn't be confused with the author's intended conclusion, but it should also be considered in the reader's final evaluation.

Text Credibility

Credible sources are important when drawing conclusions because readers need to be able to trust what they are reading. Authors should always use credible sources to help gain the trust of their readers. A text is **credible** when it is believable and the author is objective and unbiased. If readers do not trust an author's words, they may simply dismiss the text completely. For example, if an author writes a persuasive essay, they are outwardly trying to sway readers' opinions to align with their own. Readers may agree or disagree with the author, which may, in turn, lead them to believe that the author is credible or not credible. Also, readers should keep in mind the source of the text. If readers review a journal about astronomy, would a more reliable source be a NASA employee or a medical doctor? Overall, text credibility is important when drawing conclusions, because readers want reliable sources that support the decisions they have made about the author's ideas.

Examining Paragraphs

While authors write, thoughts coalesce to form words on "paper" (aka a computer screen). Authors strategically place those thoughts in sentences to give them "voice" in an orderly manner, and then they manipulate them into cohesive sentences to express ideas. Like a hunk of modeling clay, sentences can be worked and reworked until they cooperate and say what was originally intended.

Before calling a paragraph complete, identify its main point, making sure that related sentences stay on point. Pose questions such as, "Did I sufficiently develop the main point? Did I say it succinctly enough? Did I give it time to develop? *Is* it developed?"

Let's examine the following two paragraphs, each an example of a movie review. Read them and form a critique.

Example 1: *Eddie the Eagle* is a movie about a struggling athlete. Eddie was crippled at birth. He had a lot of therapy and he had a dream. Eddie trained himself for the Olympics. He went far away to learn how to ski jump. It was hard for him, but he persevered. He got a coach and kept trying. He qualified for the Olympics. He was the only one from Britain who could jump. When he succeeded, they named him, "Eddie the Eagle."

Example 2: The last movie I saw in the theater was *Eddie the Eagle,* a story of extraordinary perseverance inspired by real life events. Eddie was born in England with a birth defect that he slowly but surely overcame, but not without trial and error (not the least of which was his father's perpetual *dis*couragement). In fact, the old man did everything to get him to give up, but Eddie was dogged beyond anyone in the neighborhood; in fact, maybe beyond anyone in the whole town or even the whole world! Eddie, simply, did not know to quit. As he grew up, so did his dream; a strange one, indeed, for someone so unaccomplished: to compete in the Winter Olympics as a ski jumper (which he knew absolutely nothing about). Eddie didn't just keep on dreaming about it. He actually went to Germany and *worked* at it, facing unbelievable odds, defeats, and put-downs by Dad and the other Men in Charge, aka the Olympic decision-makers. Did that stop him? No way! Eddie got a coach and persevered. Then, when he failed, he persevered some more, again and again. You should be able to open up a dictionary, look at the word "persevere," and see a picture of Eddie the Eagle because, when everybody told him he couldn't, he did. The result? He is forever dubbed, "Eddie the Eagle."

Both reviews tell something about the movie *Eddie the Eagle*. Does one motivate the reader to want to see the movie more than the other? Does one just provide a few facts while the other paints a virtual picture of the movie? Does one give a carrot and the other a rib eye steak, mashed potatoes, and chocolate silk pie?

Paragraphs sometimes only give facts. Sometimes that's appropriate and all that is needed. Sometimes, though, writers want to use the blank documents on their computer screens to paint a picture. Writers must "see" the painting come to life. To do so, pick a familiar topic, write a simple sentence, and add to it. Pretend, for instance, there's a lovely view. What does one see? Is it a lake? Try again—picture it as though it were the sea! Visualize a big ship sailing out there. Is it sailing away or approaching? Who is on it? Is it dangerous? Is it night and are there crazy pirates on board? Uh-oh! Did one just jump ship and start swimming toward shore?

The Steps of an Argument

Strong arguments tend to follow a fairly defined format. In the introduction, background information regarding the problem is shared, the implications of the issue, and the author's thesis or claims. Supporting evidence is then presented in the body paragraphs, along with the counterargument, which then gets refuted with specific evidence. Lastly, in the conclusion, the author summarizes the points and claims again.

Evidence Used to Support a Claim or Conclusion

Premises are the why, and **conclusions** are the what. Stated differently, premises are the evidence or facts supporting why the conclusion is logical and valid. Logically-sound arguments do not require evaluation of the factual accuracy; instead, an argument's logical strength is assessed. For example, John eats all red food. Apples are red. Therefore, John eats apples. This argument is logically sound, despite having no factual basis in reality. Below is an example of a practice argument.

> Julie is an American track athlete. She's the star of the number one collegiate team in the country. Her times are consistently at the top of national rankings. Julie is extremely likely to represent the United States at the upcoming Olympics.

In this example, the conclusion, or the *what*, is that she will likely be on the American Olympic team. The author supports this conclusion with two premises. First, Julie is the star of an elite track team. Second, she runs some of the best times of the country. This is the *why* behind the conclusion. The following builds off this basic argument:

> Julie is an American track athlete. She's the star of the number one collegiate team in the country. Her times are consistently at the top of national rankings. Julie is extremely likely to represent the United States at the upcoming Olympics. Julie will continue to develop after the Olympic trials. She will be a frontrunner for the gold. Julie is likely to become a world-famous track star.

These additions to the argument make the conclusion different. Now, the conclusion is that Julie is likely to become a world-famous track star. The previous conclusion, Julie will likely be on the Olympic team, functions as a **sub-conclusion** in this argument. Like conclusions, premises must adequately support sub-conclusions. However, sub-conclusions function like premises, since sub-conclusions also support the overall conclusion.

Determining Whether Evidence is Relevant and Sufficient

A **hasty generalization** involves an argument relying on insufficient statistical data or inaccurately generalizing. One common generalization occurs when a group of individuals under observation have some quality or attribute that is asserted to be universal or true for a much larger number of people than actually documented. Here's an example of a hasty generalization:

> A man smokes a lot of cigarettes, but so did his grandfather. The grandfather smoked nearly two packs per day since his World War II service until he died at ninety years of age. Continuing to smoke cigarettes will clearly not impact the grandson's long-term health.

This argument is a hasty generalization because it assumes that one person's addiction and lack of consequences will naturally be reflected in a different individual. There is no reasonable justification for such extrapolation. It is common knowledge that any smoking is detrimental to everyone's health. The fact that the man's grandfather smoked two packs per day and lived a long life has no logical connection with the grandson engaging in similar behavior. The hasty generalization doesn't take into account other reasons behind the grandfather's longevity. Nor does the author offer evidence that might support the idea that the man would share a similar lifetime if he smokes. It might be different if the author stated that the man's family shares some genetic trait rendering them immune to the effects of tar and chemicals on the lungs. If this were in the argument, we would assume it as truth and find the generalization to be valid rather than hasty. Of course, this is not the case in our example.

Determining Whether a Statement Is or Is Not Supported

The basic tenant of reading comprehension is the ability to read and understand text. One way to understand text is to look for information that supports the author's main idea, topic, or position statement. This information may be factual, or it may be based on the author's opinion. This section will focus on the test taker's ability to identify factual information, as opposed to opinionated bias. The ACT will ask test takers to read passages containing factual information, and then logically relate those passages by drawing conclusions based on evidence.

In order to identify factual information within one or more text passages, begin by looking for statements of fact. Factual statements can be either true or false. Identifying factual statements as opposed to opinion statements is important in demonstrating full command of evidence in reading. For example, the statement *The temperature outside was unbearably hot* may seem like a fact; however, it's not. While anyone can point to a temperature gauge as factual evidence, the statement itself reflects only an opinion. Some people may find the temperature unbearably hot. Others may find it comfortably warm. Thus, the sentence, *The temperature outside was unbearably hot,* reflects the opinion of the author who found it unbearable. If the text passage followed up the sentence with atmospheric conditions indicating heat indices above 140 degrees Fahrenheit, then the reader knows there is factual information that supports the author's assertion of *unbearably hot*.

In looking for information that can be proven or disproven, it's helpful to scan for dates, numbers, timelines, equations, statistics, and other similar data within any given text passage. These types of indicators will point to proven particulars. For example, the statement, *The temperature outside was unbearably hot on that summer day, July 10, 1913,* most likely indicates factual information, even if the reader is unaware that this is the hottest day on record in the United States. Be careful when reading biased words from an author. Biased words indicate opinion, as opposed to fact.

See the list of biased words below and keep in mind that it's not an inclusive list:

- Good/bad
- Great/greatest
- Better/best/worst
- Amazing
- Terrible/bad/awful
- Beautiful/handsome/ugly
- More/most
- Exciting/dull/boring
- Favorite
- Very
- Probably/should/seem/possibly

Remember, most of what is written is actually opinion or carefully worded information that seems like fact when it isn't. To say, *duplicating DNA results is not cost-effective* sounds like it could be a scientific fact, but it isn't. Factual information can be verified through independent sources.

The simplest type of test question may provide a text passage, then ask the test taker to distinguish the correct factual supporting statement that best answers the corresponding question on the test. However, be aware that most questions may ask the test taker to read more than one text passage and identify which answer best supports an author's topic. While the ability to identify factual information is critical, these types of questions require the test taker to identify chunks of details, and then relate them to one another.

Assessing Whether an Argument is Valid

Although different from conditions and If/Then Statements, **reasonableness** is another important foundational concept. Evaluating an argument for reasonableness and validity entails evaluating the evidence presented by the author to justify their conclusions. Everything contained in the argument should be considered, but remember to ignore outside biases, judgments, and knowledge. For the purposes of this test, the test taker is a one-person jury at a criminal trial using a standard of reasonableness under the circumstances presented by the argument.

These arguments are encountered on a daily basis through social media, entertainment, and cable news. An example is:

> Although many believe it to be a natural occurrence, some believe that the red tide that occurs in Florida each year may actually be a result of human sewage and agricultural runoff. However, it is arguable that both natural and human factors contribute to this annual phenomenon. On one hand, the red tide has been occurring every year since the time of explorers like Cabeza de Vaca in the 1500's. On the other hand, the red tide seems to be getting worse each year, and scientists from the Florida Fish & Wildlife Conservation say the bacteria found inside the tide feed off of nutrients found in fertilizer runoff.

The author's conclusion is that both natural phenomena and human activity contribute to the red tide that happens annually in Florida. The author backs this information up by historical data to prove the natural occurrence of the red tide, and then again with scientific data to back up the human contribution to the red tide. Both of these statements are examples of the premises in the argument. Evaluating the strength of the logical connection between the premises and conclusion is how reasonableness is determined. Another example is:

> The local railroad is a disaster. Tickets are exorbitantly priced, bathrooms leak, and the floor is sticky.

The author is clearly unhappy with the railroad service. They cite three examples of why they believe the railroad to be a disaster. An argument more familiar to everyday life is:

> Alexandra said the movie she just saw was amazing. We should go see it tonight.

Although not immediately apparent, this is an argument. The author is making the argument that they should go see the movie. This conclusion is based on the premise that Alexandra said the movie was amazing. There's an inferred note that Alexandra is knowledgeable on the subject, and she's credible enough to prompt her friends to go see the movie. This seems like a reasonable argument. A less reasonable argument is:

> Alexandra is a film student, and she's written the perfect romantic comedy script. We should put our life savings toward its production as an investment in our future.

The author's conclusion is that they should invest their life savings into the production of a movie, and it is justified by referencing Alexandra's credibility and current work. However, the premises are entirely too weak to support the conclusion. Alexandra is only a film *student*, and the script is seemingly her first work. This is not enough evidence to justify investing one's life savings in the film's success.

Assumptions in an Argument

Think of assumptions as unwritten premises. Although they never explicitly appear in the argument, the author is relying on it to defend the argument, just like a premise. Assumptions are the most important part of an argument that will never appear in an argument.

An argument in the abstract is: The author concludes Z based on W and X premises. But the W and X premises actually depend on the unmentioned assumption of Y. Therefore, what the author is really saying is that, X, W, and Y make Z correct, but Y is assumed.

People assume all of the time. Assumptions and inferences allow the human mind to process the constant flow of information. Many assumptions underlie even the most basic arguments. However, in the world of Legal Reasoning arguments, assumptions must be avoided. An argument must be fully presented to be valid; relying on an assumption is considered weak. The test requires that test takers identify these underlying assumptions. One example is:

> Peyton Manning is the most over-rated quarterback of all time. He lost more big games than anyone else. Plus, he allegedly assaulted his female trainer in college. Peyton clearly shouldn't make the Hall of Fame.

The author relies on a lot of assumptions. A few assumptions are:

- Peyton Manning plays quarterback.
- He is considered to be a great quarterback by at least some people.
- He played in many big games.
- Allegations and past settlements from over a decade ago can be relied upon as evidence against Hall of Fame acceptance.
- The Hall of Fame voters factor in off-the-field incidents.
- The best players should make the Hall of Fame.
- Losing big games negates, at least in part, the achievement of making it to those big games.
- Peyton Manning is retired, and people will vote on whether he makes the Hall of Fame at some point in the future.

The author is relying on all of these assumptions. Some are clearly more important to the argument than others. In fact, disproving a necessary assumption can destroy a premise and possibly an entire conclusion. For example, what if the Hall of Fame did not factor in any of the off-the-field incidents? Then the alleged assault no longer factors into the argument. Even worse, what if making the big games actually was more important than losing those games in the eyes of the Hall of Fame voters? Then the whole conclusion falls apart. The conclusion is no longer justified if that premise is disproven.

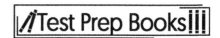

If the author truly relies on an assumption, then the argument will completely fall apart if the assumption isn't true. **Negating** a necessary assumption will *always* make the argument fall apart. This is a universal rule of logic and should be the first thing done in testing answer choices.

Analyzing Two Arguments and Evaluating the Types of Evidence Used to Support Each Claim

Arguments use evidence and reasoning to support a position or prove a point. Claims are typically controversial and may be faced with some degree of contention. Thus, authors support claims with evidence. Two arguments might present different types of evidence that readers will need to evaluate for merit, worthiness, accuracy, relevance, and impact. Evidence can take on many forms such as numbers (statistics, measurements, numerical data, etc.), expert opinions or quotes, testimonies, anecdotal evidence or stories from individuals, and textual evidence, such as that obtained from documents like diaries, newspapers, and laws.

Writing an Essay

Brainstorming

One of the most important steps in writing an essay is prewriting. Before drafting an essay, it's helpful to think about the topic for a moment or two, in order to gain a more solid understanding of what the task is. Then, spending about five minutes jotting down the immediate ideas that could work for the essay is recommended. It is a way to get some words on the page and offer a reference for ideas when drafting. Scratch paper is provided for writers to use any prewriting techniques such as webbing, free writing, or listing. The goal is to get ideas out of the mind and onto the page.

Considering Opposing Viewpoints

In the planning stage, it's important to consider all aspects of the topic, including different viewpoints on the subject. There are more than two ways to look at a topic, and a strong argument considers those opposing viewpoints. Considering opposing viewpoints can help writers present a fair, balanced, and informed essay that shows consideration for all readers. This approach can also strengthen an argument by recognizing and potentially refuting the opposing viewpoint(s).

Drawing from personal experience may help to support ideas. For example, if the goal for writing is a personal narrative, then the story should be from the writer's own life. Many writers find it helpful to draw from personal experience, even in an essay that is not strictly narrative. Personal anecdotes or short stories can help to illustrate a point in other types of essays as well.

Moving from Brainstorming to Planning

Once the ideas are on the page, it's time to turn them into a solid plan for the essay. The best ideas from the brainstorming results can then be developed into a more formal outline. An outline typically has one main point (the thesis) and at least three sub-points that support the main point. Here's an example:

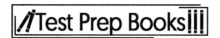

Main Idea

- Point #1
- Point #2
- Point #3

Of course, there will be details under each point, but this approach is the best for dealing with timed writing.

Staying on Track

Basing the essay on the outline aids in both organization and coherence. The goal is to ensure that there is enough time to develop each sub-point in the essay, roughly spending an equal amount of time on each idea. Keeping an eye on the time will help. If there are fifteen minutes left to draft the essay, then it makes sense to spend about 5 minutes on each of the ideas. Staying on task is critical to success, and timing out the parts of the essay can help writers avoid feeling overwhelmed.

Parts of the Essay

The **introduction** has to do a few important things:

- Establish the topic of the essay in original wording (i.e., not just repeating the prompt)
- Clarify the significance/importance of the topic or purpose for writing (not too many details, a brief overview)
- Offer a thesis statement that identifies the writer's own viewpoint on the topic (typically one-two brief sentences as a clear, concise explanation of the main point on the topic)

Body paragraphs reflect the ideas developed in the outline. Three-four points is probably sufficient for a short essay, and they should include the following:

- A topic sentence that identifies the sub-point (e.g., a reason why, a way how, a cause or effect)
- A detailed explanation of the point, explaining why the writer thinks this point is valid
- Illustrative examples, such as personal examples or real-world examples, that support and validate the point (i.e., "prove" the point)
- A concluding sentence that connects the examples, reasoning, and analysis to the point being made

The **conclusion**, or final paragraph, should be brief and should reiterate the focus, clarifying why the discussion is significant or important. It is important to avoid adding specific details or new ideas to this paragraph. The purpose of the conclusion is to sum up what has been said to bring the discussion to a close.

Passage Development

Transition Words

The writer should act as a guide, showing the reader how all the sentences fit together. Consider this example:

> Seat belts save more lives than any other automobile safety feature. Many studies show that airbags save lives as well. Not all cars have airbags. Many older cars don't. Air bags aren't entirely reliable. Studies show that in 15% of accidents, airbags don't deploy as designed. Seat belt malfunctions are extremely rare.

There's nothing wrong with any of these sentences individually, but together they're disjointed and difficult to follow. The best way for the writer to communicate information is through the use of transition words. Here are examples of transition words and phrases that tie sentences together, enabling a more natural flow:

- To show causality: *as a result, therefore,* and *consequently*
- To compare and contrast: *however, but,* and *on the other hand*
- To introduce examples: *for instance, namely,* and *including*
- To show order of importance: *foremost, primarily, secondly,* and *lastly*

NOTE: This is not a complete list of transitions. There are many more that can be used; however, most fit into these or similar categories. The point is that the words should clearly show the relationship between sentences, supporting information, and the main idea.

Here is an update to the previous example using transition words. These changes make it easier to read and bring clarity to the writer's points:

> Seat belts save more lives than any other automobile safety feature. Many studies show that airbags save lives as well; however, not all cars have airbags. For instance, some older cars don't. Furthermore, air bags aren't entirely reliable. For example, studies show that in 15% of accidents, airbags don't deploy as designed; but, on the other hand, seat belt malfunctions are extremely rare.

Also, be prepared to analyze whether the writer is using the best transition word or phrase for the situation. Take this sentence for example: "As a result, seat belt malfunctions are extremely rare." This sentence doesn't make sense in the context above because the writer is trying to show the contrast between seat belts and airbags, not the causality.

Logical Sequence

Even if the writer includes plenty of information to support their point, the writing is only coherent when the information is in a logical order. **Logical sequencing** is really just common sense, but it's an important writing technique. First, the writer should introduce the main idea, whether for a paragraph, a section, or the entire piece. Then they should present evidence to support the main idea by using transitional language. This shows the reader how the information relates to the main idea and the sentences around it. The writer should then take time to interpret the information, making sure necessary connections are obvious to the reader. Finally, the writer can summarize the information in a closing section.

NOTE: Though most writing follows this pattern, it isn't a set rule. Sometimes writers change the order for effect. For example, the writer can begin with a surprising piece of supporting information to grab the reader's attention, and then transition to the main idea. Thus, if a passage doesn't follow the logical order, don't immediately assume it's wrong. However, most writing usually settles into a logical sequence after a nontraditional beginning.

Precision

People often think of precision in terms of math, but precise word choice is another key to successful writing. Since language itself is imprecise, it's important for the writer to find the exact word or words to convey the full, intended meaning of a given situation. For example:

> The number of deaths has gone down since seat belt laws started.

There are several problems with this sentence. First, the word *deaths* is too general. From the context, it's assumed that the writer is referring only to deaths caused by car accidents. However, without clarification, the sentence lacks impact and is probably untrue. The phrase *gone down* might be accurate, but a more precise word would provide more information and greater accuracy. Did the numbers show a slow and steady decrease in highway fatalities or a sudden drop? If the latter is true, the writer is missing a chance to make the point more dramatically. Instead of *gone down* the author could substitute *plummeted*, *fallen drastically*, or *rapidly diminished* to bring the information to life. Also, the phrase *seat belt laws* is unclear. Does it refer to laws requiring cars to include seat belts or to laws requiring drivers and passengers to use them? Finally, *started* is not a strong verb. Words like *enacted* or *adopted* are more direct and make the content more real. When put together, these changes create a far more powerful sentence:

> The number of highway fatalities has plummeted since laws requiring seat belt usage were enacted.

However, it's important to note that precise word choice can sometimes be taken too far. If the writer of the sentence above takes precision to an extreme, it might result in the following:

> The incidence of high-speed, automobile accident-related fatalities has decreased 75% and continued to remain at historical lows since the initial set of federal legislations requiring seat belt use were enacted in 1992.

This sentence is extremely precise, but it takes so long to achieve that precision that it suffers from a lack of clarity. Precise writing is about finding the right balance between information and flow. This is also an issue of conciseness (discussed in the next section).

The last thing for writers to consider with precision is a word choice that's not only unclear or uninteresting, but also confusing or misleading. For example:

> The number of highway fatalities has become hugely lower since laws requiring seat belt use were enacted.

In this case, the reader might be confused by the word *hugely*. Huge means large, but here the writer uses *hugely* in an incorrect and awkward manner. Although most readers can decipher this, doing so disconnects them from the flow of the writing and makes the writer's point less effective.

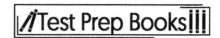

Concision

"Less is more" is a good rule for writers to follow when composing a sentence. Unfortunately, writers often include extra words and phrases that seem necessary at the time but add nothing to the main idea. This confuses the reader and creates unnecessary repetition. Writing that lacks conciseness is usually guilty of excessive wordiness and redundant phrases. Here's an example containing both of these issues:

> When legislators decided to begin creating legislation making it mandatory for automobile drivers and passengers to make use of seat belts while in cars, a large number of them made those laws for reasons that were political reasons.

There are several empty or "fluff" words here that take up too much space. These can be eliminated while still maintaining the writer's meaning. For example:

- *decided* to begin could be shortened to began
- *making it mandatory for* could be shortened to requiring
- *make use of* could be shortened to use
- *a large number* could be shortened to many

In addition, there are several examples of redundancy that can be eliminated:

- *legislators decided to begin creating legislation* and *made those laws*
- *automobile drivers and passengers* and *while in cars*
- *reasons that were political reasons*

These changes are incorporated as follows:

> When legislators began requiring drivers and passengers to use seat belts, many of them did so for political reasons.

There are many general examples of redundant phrases, such as *add an additional, complete and total, time schedule,* and *transportation vehicle.* If asked to identify a redundant phrase on the exam, test takers should look for words that are close together with the same (or similar) meanings.

Don't Panic!

Writing an essay can be overwhelming, and performance panic is a natural response. The outline serves as a basis for the writing and helps writers keep focused. Getting stuck can also happen, and it's helpful to remember that brainstorming can be done at any time during the writing process. Following the steps of the writing process is the best defense against writer's block.

Timed essays can be particularly stressful, but assessors are trained to recognize the necessary planning and thinking for these timed efforts. Using the plan above and sticking to it helps with time management. Timing each part of the process helps writers stay on track. Sometimes writers try to cover too much in their essays. If time seems to be running out, this is an opportunity to determine whether all of the ideas in the outline are necessary. Three body paragraphs are sufficient, and more than that is probably too much to cover in a short essay.

More isn't always *better* in writing. A strong essay will be clear and concise. It will avoid unnecessary or repetitive details. It is better to have a concise, five-paragraph essay that makes a clear point, than a ten-paragraph essay that doesn't. The goal is to write one to two pages of quality writing. Paragraphs should also reflect balance; if the introduction goes to the bottom of the first page, the writing may be going off-track or be repetitive. It's best to fall into the one-to-two page range, but a complete, well-developed essay is the ultimate goal.

The Final Steps

Leaving a few minutes at the end to revise and proofread offers an opportunity for writers to polish things up. Putting one's self in the reader's shoes and focusing on what the essay actually says helps writers identify problems—it's a movement from the mindset of writer to the mindset of editor. The goal is to have a clean, clear copy of the essay. The following areas should be considered when proofreading:

- Sentence fragments
- Awkward sentence structure
- Run-on sentences
- Incorrect word choice
- Grammatical agreement errors
- Spelling errors
- Punctuation errors
- Capitalization errors

The Short Overview

The essay may seem challenging, but following these steps can help writers focus:

- Take one or two minutes to think about the topic.
- Generate some ideas through brainstorming (three or four minutes).
- Organize ideas into a brief outline, selecting just three or four main points to cover in the essay (eventually the body paragraphs).
- Develop essay in parts:
  - Introduction paragraph, with intro to topic and main points
  - Viewpoint on the subject at the end of the introduction
  - Body paragraphs, based on outline
  - Each paragraph: makes a main point, explains the viewpoint, uses examples to support the point
  - Brief conclusion highlighting the main points and closing
- Read over the essay (last five minutes).
- Look for any obvious errors, making sure that the writing makes sense.

Standard Conventions in English

Word Parts

By analyzing and understanding Latin, Greek, and Anglo-Saxon word roots, prefixes, and suffixes, one can better understand word meanings. Of course, people can always look words up in a dictionary or

thesaurus if available, but meaning can often be gleaned on the spot if the reader learns to dissect and examine words.

A word can consist of the following combinations:

- root
- root + suffix
- prefix + root
- prefix + root + suffix

For example, if someone was unfamiliar with the word *submarine* they could break the word into its parts.

- prefix + root
- sub + marine

It can be determined that *sub* means *below* as in *subway* and *subpar*. Additionally, one can determine that *marine* refers to *the sea* as in *marine life*. Thus, it can be figured that *submarine* refers to something below the water.

Roots

Roots are the basic components of words. Many roots can stand alone as individual words, but others must be combined with a prefix or suffix to be a word. For example, *calc* is a root but it needs a suffix to be an actual word (*calcium*).

Prefixes

A **prefix** is a word, letter, or number that is placed before another. It adjusts or qualifies the root word's meaning. When written alone, prefixes are followed by a dash to indicate that the root word follows. Some of the most common prefixes are the following:

Prefix	Meaning	Example
dis-	not or opposite of	disabled
in-, im-, il-, ir-	not	illiterate
re-	again	return
un-	not	unpredictable
anti-	against	antibacterial
fore-	before	forefront
mis-	wrongly	misunderstand
non-	not	nonsense
over-	more than normal	overabundance
pre-	before	preheat
super-	above	superman

Suffixes

A **suffix** is a letter or group of letters added at the end of a word to form another word. The word created from the root and suffix is either a different tense of the same root (*help* + *ed* = *helped*) or a new word (*help* + *ful* = *helpful*). When written alone, suffixes are preceded by a dash to indicate that the root word comes before.

Some of the most common suffixes are the following:

Suffix	Meaning	Example
-ed	makes a verb past tense	washed
-ing	makes a verb a present participle verb	washing
-ly	to make characteristic of	lovely
-s, -es	to make more than one	chairs, boxes
-able	can be done	deplorable
-al	having characteristics of	comical
-est	comparative	greatest
-ful	full of	wonderful
-ism	belief in	communism
-less	without	faithless
-ment	action or process	accomplishment
-ness	state of	happiness
-ize, -ise	to render, to make	sterilize, advertise
-cede, -ceed, -sede	go	concede, proceed, supersede

Here are some helpful tips:

- When adding a suffix that starts with a vowel (for example, -*ed*) to a one-syllable root whose vowel has a short sound and ends in a consonant (for example, stun), the final consonant of the root (*n*) gets doubled.

  o *stun* + *ed* = stunned

  o Exception: If the past tense verb ends in *x* such as *box*, the *x* does not get doubled.

  o *box* + *ed* = boxed

- If adding a suffix that starts with a vowel (-*er*) to a multi-syllable word ending in a consonant (*begin*), the consonant (*n*) is doubled.

  o *begin* + *er* = beginner

- If a short vowel is followed by two or more consonants in a word such as *i+t+c+h* = itch, the last consonant should not be doubled.

  o *itch* + *ed* = itched

- If adding a suffix that starts with a vowel (-*ing*) to a word ending in e (for example, *name*), that word's final e is generally (but not always) dropped.

  o *name* + *ing* = naming

  o exception: *manage* + *able* = manageable

- If adding a suffix that starts with a consonant (*-ness*) to a word ending in *e* (*complete*), the *e* generally (but not always) remains.

  o *complete* + *ness* = completeness

  o exception: *judge* + *ment* = judgment

- There is great diversity on handling words that end in *y*. For words ending in a vowel + *y*, nothing changes in the original word.

  o *play* + *ed* = played

- For words ending in a consonant + *y*, the y is changed to *i* when adding any suffix except for *-ing*.

  o *marry* + *ed* = married

  o *marry* + *ing* = marrying

Syntax

Syntax refers to the arrangement of words, phrases, and clauses to form a sentence. Knowledge of syntax can also give insight into a word's meaning. Here is an example of how the placement of a word can impact its meaning and grammatical function:

The development team has reserved the conference room for today.

Her quiet and reserved nature is sometimes misinterpreted as unfriendliness when people first meet her.

In addition to using *reserved* to mean different things, each sentence also uses the word to serve a different grammatical function. In sentence A, *reserved* is part of the verb phrase *has reserved*, indicating the meaning "to set aside for a particular use." In sentence B, *reserved* acts as a modifier within the noun phrase "her quiet and reserved nature." Because the word is being used as an adjective to describe a personality characteristic, it calls up a different definition of the word—"restrained or lacking familiarity with others." As this example shows, the function of a word within the overall sentence structure can allude to its meaning.

Sentence Structure and Formation

Sentence Structure
Simple sentence: composed of one independent clause

Many people watch hummingbirds.

Note that it has one subject and one verb; however, a simple sentence can have a compound subject and/or a compound verb.

Adults and children often enjoy watching and photographing hummingbirds.

Compound sentence: composed of two independent clauses

The wind knocked down lots of trees, but no trees in my yard were affected.

Complex sentence: composed of one independent clause and one dependent clause

> Although the wind knocked down lots of trees, no trees in my yard were affected.

Sentence Fluency

Learning and utilizing the mechanics of structure will encourage effective, professional results, and adding some creativity will elevate one's writing to a higher level.

First, the basic elements of sentences will be reviewed.

A **sentence** is a set of words that make up a grammatical unit. The words must have certain elements and be spoken or written in a specific order to constitute a complete sentence that makes sense.

- A sentence must have a **subject** (a noun or noun phrase). The subject tells whom or what the sentence is addressing (i.e. what it is about).

- A sentence must have an **action** or **state of being** (a verb). To reiterate: A verb forms the main part of the predicate of a sentence. This means that it explains what the noun is doing.

- A sentence must convey a complete thought.

When examining writing, readers should be mindful of grammar, structure, spelling, and patterns. Sentences can come in varying sizes and shapes, so the point of grammatical correctness is not to stamp out creativity or diversity in writing. Rather, grammatical correctness ensures that writing will be enjoyable and clear. One of the most common methods successful test takers employ to catch errors is to mouth the words as they read them. Many typos are fixed automatically by the brain, but mouthing the words often circumvents this instinct and helps one read what's actually on the page. Often, grammar errors are caught not by memorization of grammar rules but by the training of one's mind to know whether something *sounds* right or not.

Types of Sentences

There isn't an overabundance of absolutes in grammar, but here is one: every sentence in the English language falls into one of four categories.

Declarative: a simple statement that ends with a period

> The price of milk per gallon is the same as the price of gasoline.

Imperative: a command, instruction, or request that ends with a period

> Buy milk when you stop to fill up your car with gas.

Interrogative: a question that ends with a question mark

> Will you buy the milk?

Exclamatory: a statement or command that expresses emotions like anger, urgency, or surprise and ends with an exclamation mark

> Buy the milk now!

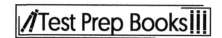

Declarative sentences are the most common type, probably because they are comprised of the most general content, without any of the bells and whistles that the other three types contain. They are, simply, declarations or statements of any degree of seriousness, importance, or information.

Imperative sentences often seem to be missing a subject. The subject is there, though; it is just not visible or audible because it is *implied*. For example:

Buy the milk when you fill up your car with gas.

In this sentence, *you* is the implied subject, the one to whom the command is issued. This is sometimes called *the understood you* because it is understood that *you* is the subject of the sentence.

Interrogative sentences—those that ask questions—are defined as such from the idea of the word **interrogation**, the action of questions being asked of suspects by investigators. Although that is serious business, interrogative sentences apply to all kinds of questions.

To exclaim is at the root of **exclamatory** sentences. These are made with strong emotions behind them. The only technical difference between a declarative or imperative sentence and an exclamatory one is the exclamation mark at the end. The example declarative and imperative sentences can both become an exclamatory one simply by putting an exclamation mark at the end of the sentences.

The price of milk per gallon is the same as the price of gasoline!

Buy milk when you stop to fill up your car with gas!

After all, someone might be really excited by the price of gas or milk, or they could be mad at the person that will be buying the milk! However, as stated before, exclamation marks in abundance defeat their own purpose! After a while, they begin to cause fatigue! When used only for their intended purpose, they can have their expected and desired effect.

Transitions

Transitions are the glue use to make organized thoughts adhere to one another. Transitions are the glue that helps put ideas together seamlessly, within sentences and paragraphs, between them, and (in longer documents) even between sections. Transitions may be single words, sentences, or whole paragraphs (as in the prior example). Transitions help readers to digest and understand what to feel about what has gone on and clue readers in on what is going on, what will be, and how they might react to all these factors. Transitions are like good clues left at a crime scene.

Parallel Structure in a Sentence

Parallel structure, also known as **parallelism**, refers to using the same grammatical form within a sentence. This is important in lists and for other components of sentences.

Incorrect: At the recital, the boys and girls were dancing, singing, and played musical instruments.

Correct: At the recital, the boys and girls were dancing, singing, and playing musical instruments.

Notice that in the first example, *played* is not in the same verb tense as the other verbs nor is it compatible with the helping verb *were*. To test for parallel structure in lists, try reading each item as if it were the only item in the list.

> The boys and girls were dancing.

> The boys and girls were singing.

> The boys and girls were played musical instruments.

Suddenly, the error in the sentence becomes very clear. Here's another example:

Incorrect: After the accident, I informed the police *that Mrs. Holmes backed* into my car, *that Mrs. Holmes got out* of her car to look at the damage, and *she was driving* off without leaving a note.

Correct: After the accident, I informed the police *that Mrs. Holmes backed* into my car, *that Mrs. Holmes got out* of her car to look at the damage, and *that Mrs. Holmes drove off* without leaving a note.

Correct: After the accident, I informed the police that Mrs. Holmes *backed* into my car, *got out* of her car to look at the damage, and *drove off* without leaving a note.

Note that there are two ways to fix the nonparallel structure of the first sentence. The key to parallelism is consistent structure.

Punctuation

Ellipses

An **ellipsis** (. . .) consists of three handy little dots that can speak volumes on behalf of irrelevant material. Writers use them in place of words, lines, phrases, list content, or paragraphs that might just as easily have been omitted from a passage of writing. This can be done to save space or to focus only on the specifically relevant material.

> Exercise is good for some unexpected reasons. Watkins writes, "Exercise has many benefits such as . . . reducing cancer risk."

In the example above, the ellipsis takes the place of the other benefits of exercise that are more expected.

The ellipsis may also be used to show a pause in sentence flow.

> "I'm wondering . . . how this could happen," Dylan said in a soft voice.

Commas

A **comma** (,) is the punctuation mark that signifies a pause—breath—between parts of a sentence. It denotes a break of flow. As with so many aspects of writing structure, authors will benefit by reading their writing aloud or mouthing the words. This can be particularly helpful if one is uncertain about whether the comma is needed.

In a complex sentence—one that contains a **subordinate (dependent)** clause or clauses—the use of a comma is dictated by where the subordinate clause is located. If the subordinate clause is located before the main clause, a comma is needed between the two clauses.

I will not pay for the steak, *because I don't have that much money.*

Generally, if the subordinate clause is placed after the main clause, no punctuation is needed.

I did well on my exam because I studied two hours the night before.

Notice how the last clause is dependent because it requires the earlier independent clause to make sense.

Use a comma on both sides of an interrupting phrase.

I am, *as you can probably tell,* really excited about the beach.

The words forming the phrase in italics are nonessential (extra) information. To determine if a phrase is nonessential, try reading the sentence without the phrase and see if it's still coherent.

A comma is not necessary in this next sentence because no interruption—nonessential or extra information—has occurred. Read sentences aloud when uncertain.

I will pay for his chocolate and vanilla ice cream and then will eat it all myself.

If the nonessential phrase comes at the beginning of a sentence, a comma should only go at the end of the phrase. If the phrase comes at the end of a sentence, a comma should only go at the beginning of the phrase.

Other types of interruptions include the following:

- Interjections: Oh no, I am not going.
- Abbreviations: Barry Potter, M.D., specializes in heart disorders.
- Direct addresses: Yes, Claudia, I am tired and going to bed.
- Parenthetical phrases: His coworker, friendly as he was, was not helpful.
- Transitional phrases: Also, it is not possible.

The second comma in the following sentence is called an Oxford comma.

I will pay for ice cream, syrup, and pop.

It is a comma used after the second-to-last item in a series of three or more items. It comes before the word *or* or *and*. Not everyone uses the Oxford comma; it is optional, but many believe it is needed. The comma functions as a tool to reduce confusion in writing. So, if omitting the Oxford comma would cause confusion, then it's best to include it.

Commas are used in math to mark the place of thousands in numerals, breaking them up so they are easier to read. Other uses for commas are in dates (*March 19, 2016*), letter greetings (*Dear Sally,*), and in between cities and states (*Louisville, KY*).

Semicolons

The **semicolon** (;) might be described as a heavy-handed comma. Take a look at these two examples:

I will pay for the ice cream, but I will not pay for the steak.

I will pay for the ice cream; I will not pay for the steak.

What's the difference? The first example has a comma and a conjunction separating the two independent clauses. The second example does not have a conjunction, but there are two independent clauses in the sentence, so something more than a comma is required. In this case, a semicolon is used.

Two independent clauses can only be joined in a sentence by either a comma and conjunction or a semicolon. If one of those tools is not used, the sentence will be a run-on. Remember that while the clauses are independent, they need to be closely related in order to be contained in one sentence.

Another use for the semicolon is to separate items in a list when the items themselves require commas.

The family lived in Phoenix, Arizona; Oklahoma City, Oklahoma; and Raleigh, North Carolina.

Colons

Colons (:) have many miscellaneous functions. Colons can be used to precede further information or a list. In these cases, a colon should only follow an independent clause.

Humans take in sensory information through five basic senses: sight, hearing, smell, touch, and taste.

The meal includes the following components:

- Caesar salad
- Spaghetti
- Garlic bread
- Cake

The family got what they needed: a reliable vehicle.

While a comma is more common, a colon can also proceed a formal quotation.

He said to the crowd: "Let's begin!"

The colon is used after the greeting in a formal letter.

Dear Sir:

To Whom It May Concern:

In the writing of time, the colon separates the minutes from the hour (*4:45 p.m.*). The colon can also be used to indicate a ratio between two numbers (*50:1*).

Hyphens

The **hyphen** (-) is a little hash mark that can be used to join words to show that they are linked.

Hyphenate two words that work together as a single adjective (a compound adjective).

> honey-covered biscuits

Some words always require hyphens, even if not serving as an adjective.

> merry-go-round

Hyphens always go after certain prefixes like *anti-* & *all-*.

Hyphens should also be used when the absence of the hyphen would cause a strange vowel combination (*semi-engineer*) or confusion. For example, *re-collect* should be used to describe something being gathered twice rather than being written as *recollect*, which means to remember.

Parentheses and Dashes

Parentheses are half-round brackets that look like this: *( )*. They set off a word, phrase, or sentence that is an afterthought, explanation, or side note relevant to the surrounding text but not essential. A pair of commas is often used to set off this sort of information, but parentheses are generally used for information that would not fit well within a sentence or that the writer deems not important enough to be structurally part of the sentence.

> The picture of the heart (see above) shows the major parts you should memorize.

> Mount Everest is one of three mountains in the world that are over 28,000 feet high (K2 and Kanchenjunga are the other two).

See how the sentences above are complete without the parenthetical statements? In the first example, *see above* would not fit well within the flow of the sentence. The second parenthetical statement could have been a separate sentence, but the writer deemed the information not pertinent to the topic.

The **em-dash** (—) is a mark longer than a hyphen used as a punctuation mark in sentences and to set apart a relevant thought. Even after plucking out the line separated by the dash marks, the sentence will be intact and make sense.

> Looking out the airplane window at the landmarks—Lake Clarke, Thompson Community College, and the bridge—she couldn't help but feel excited to be home.

The dashes use is similar to that of parentheses or a pair of commas. So, what's the difference? Many believe that using dashes makes the clause within them stand out while using parentheses is subtler. It's advised to not use dashes when commas could be used instead.

Quotation Marks

Here are some instances where **quotation marks** should be used:

- Dialogue for characters in narratives. When characters speak, the first word should always be capitalized, and the punctuation goes inside the quotes. For example:
  - Janie said, "The tree fell on my car during the hurricane."
- Around titles of songs, short stories, essays, and chapter in books

- To emphasize a certain word
- To refer to a word as the word itself

Apostrophes

This punctuation mark, the apostrophe ('), is a versatile mark. It has a few different functions:

- Quotes: Apostrophes are used when a second quote is needed within a quote.

  - In my letter to my friend, I wrote, "The girl had to get a new purse, and guess what Mary did? She said, 'I'd like to go with you to the store.' I knew Mary would buy it for her."

- Contractions: Another use for an apostrophe in the quote above is a contraction. "I'd" is used for "I would."

- Possession: An apostrophe followed by the letter *s* shows possession (*Mary's purse*). If the possessive word is plural, the apostrophe generally just follows the word.

  - The trees' leaves are all over the ground.

Usage

Misspellings reduce a writer's credibility and can create misunderstandings. Spellcheckers built into word processors are not a substitute for accuracy. They are neither foolproof nor without error. In addition, a writer's misspelling of one word may also be a valid (but incorrect) word. For example, a writer intending to spell *herd* might accidentally type *s* instead of *d* and unintentionally spell *hers*. Since *her*s is a word, it would not be marked as a misspelling by a spellchecker. In short, writers should use spellcheck but not rely on it.

Guidelines for Spelling

Saying and listening to a word serves as the beginning of knowing how to spell it. Writers should keep these subsequent guidelines in mind, remembering there are often exceptions because the English language is replete with them.

Guideline #1: Syllables must have at least one vowel. In fact, every syllable in every English word has a vowel.

- d*o*g
- h*a*yst*a*ck
- *a*nsw*e*r*i*ng
- *a*bst*e*nt*iou*s
- s*i*mpl*e*

Guideline #2: The long and short of it. When the vowel has a short vowel sound as in *mad* or *bed,* only the single vowel is needed. If the word has a long vowel sound, add another vowel, either alongside it or separated by a consonant: bed/*bead*; mad/*made.* When the second vowel is separated by two consonants— *madder*—it does not affect the first vowel's sound.

Guideline #3: Suffixes. Refer to the examples listed above.

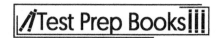

Guideline #4: Which comes first; the *i* or the *e*? Remember the saying, "*I* before *e* except after *c* or when sounding as *a* as in *neighbor* or *weigh*." Keep in mind that these are only guidelines and that there are always exceptions to every rule.

Guideline #5: Vowels in the right order. Another helpful rhyme is, "When two vowels go walking, the first one does the talking." When two vowels are in a row, the first one often has a long vowel sound and the other is silent. An example is *team*.

If one has difficulty spelling words, he or she can determine a strategy to help. Some people work on spelling by playing word games like Scrabble or Words with Friends. Others use phonics, which is sounding words out by slowly and surely stating each syllable. People try repeating and memorizing spellings as well as picturing words in their head, or they may try making up silly memory aids. Each person should experiment and see what works best.

Homophones

Homophones are two or more words that have no particular relationship to one another except their identical pronunciations. Homophones make spelling English words fun and challenging. Examples include:

Common Homophones
affect, effect
allot, a lot
barbecue, barbeque
bite, byte
brake, break
capital, capitol
cash, cache
cell, sell
colonel, kernel
do, due, dew
dual, duel
eminent, imminent
flew, flu, flue
gauge, gage
holy, wholly
it's, its
knew, new
libel, liable
principal, principle
their, there, they're
to, too, two
yoke, yolk

Irregular Plurals

Irregular plurals are words that aren't made plural the usual way.

- Most nouns are made plural by adding –s (book*s*, television*s*, skyscraper*s*).
- Most nouns ending in *ch, sh, s, x,* or *z* are made plural by adding –*es* (church*es*, marsh*es*).
- Most nouns ending in a vowel + *y* are made plural by adding –s (day*s*, toy*s*).
- Most nouns ending in a consonant + *y*, are made plural by the -*y* becoming -*ies* (baby becomes *babies*).
- Most nouns ending in an *o* are made plural by adding –s (piano*s*, photo*s*).
- Some nouns ending in an *o*, though, may be made plural by adding –*es* (example: potato*es*, volcano*es*), and, of note, there is no known rhyme or reason for this!
- Most nouns ending in an *f* or *fe* are made plural by the -*f* or -*fe* becoming -*ves*! (example: wolf becomes *wolves*).
- Some words function as both the singular and plural form of the word (fish, deer).
- Other exceptions include *man* becomes *men, mouse* becomes *mice, goose* becomes *geese*, and *foot* becomes *feet.*

Contractions

The basic rule for making **contractions** is one area of spelling that is pretty straightforward: combine the two words by inserting an apostrophe (') in the space where a letter is omitted. For example, to combine *you* and *are*, drop the *a* and put the apostrophe in its place: *you're.*

he + is = he's

you + all = y'all (informal, but often misspelled)

Note that *it's*, when spelled with an apostrophe, is always the contraction for *it is*. The possessive form of the word is written without an apostrophe as *its*.

Sample Free-Response Question

Prompt

Choose a novel wrestles with the theme of identity. Write an essay in which you analyze a specific part of identity portrayed in the novel and how the author uses a character or characters in order to explore identity. Explain how identity within society lends to the meaning of the work.

Avoid plot summary.

You may base your essay on **one** of the following works or choose another of comparable literary quality.

Their Eyes Were Watching God	Invisible Man
Little Women	Great Expectations
Kim	Surfacing
The Song of the Lark	As I Lay Dying
Bless Me, Ultima	Slaughterhouse Five
Never Let Me Go	Orlando
Persepolis	Daughter of Fortune
Alice's Adventures in Wonderland	All the Pretty Horses
Norwegian Wood	Beloved
Madame Bovary	Normal People
Demian	The Bell Jar
White Teeth	The Autobiography of an Ex-Coloured Man
Autumn of the Patriarch	The Catcher in the Rye
Go Tell It on the Mountain	The Color Purple
To Kill a Mockingbird	Main Street
I Know Why the Caged Bird Sings	Summer of My German Soldier
The Sun Also Rises	Brave New World
Things Fall Apart	Half of a Yellow Sun

Practice Test

Multiple-Choice Questions

Questions 1–12 are based on the following passage:

As long ago as 1860 it was the proper thing to be born at home. At present, so I am told, the high gods of medicine have decreed that the first cries of the young shall be uttered upon the anesthetic air of a hospital, preferably a fashionable one. So young Mr. and Mrs. Roger Button were fifty years ahead of style when they decided, one day in the summer of 1860, that their first baby should be born in a hospital. Whether this anachronism had any bearing upon the astonishing history I am about to set down will never be known.

I shall tell you what occurred, and let you judge for yourself.

The Roger Buttons held an enviable position, both social and financial, in ante-bellum Baltimore. They were related to the This Family and the That Family, which, as every Southerner knew, entitled them to membership in that enormous peerage which largely populated the Confederacy. This was their first experience with the charming old custom of having babies—Mr. Button was naturally nervous. He hoped it would be a boy so that he could be sent to Yale College in Connecticut, at which institution Mr. Button himself had been known for four years by the somewhat obvious nickname of "Cuff."

On the September morning <u>consecrated</u> to the enormous event he arose nervously at six o'clock, dressed himself, adjusted an impeccable stock, and hurried forth through the streets of Baltimore to the hospital, to determine whether the darkness of the night had borne in new life upon its bosom.

When he was approximately a hundred yards from the Maryland Private Hospital for Ladies and Gentlemen he saw Doctor Keene, the family physician, descending the front steps, rubbing his hands together with a washing movement—as all doctors are required to do by the unwritten ethics of their profession.

Mr. Roger Button, the president of Roger Button & Co., Wholesale Hardware, began to run toward Doctor Keene with much less dignity than was expected from a Southern gentleman of that picturesque period. "Doctor Keene!" he called. "Oh, Doctor Keene!"

The doctor heard him, faced around, and stood waiting, a curious expression settling on his harsh, medicinal face as Mr. Button drew near.

"What happened?" demanded Mr. Button, as he came up in a gasping rush. "What was it? How is she? A boy? Who is it? What—"

"Talk sense!" said Doctor Keene sharply. He appeared somewhat irritated.

"Is the child born?" begged Mr. Button.

Doctor Keene frowned. "Why, yes, I suppose so—after a fashion." Again he threw a curious glance at Mr. Button.

From The Curious Case of Benjamin Button by F.S. Fitzgerald, 1922.

1. According to the passage, what major event is about to happen in this story?
   a. Mr. Button is about to go to a funeral.
   b. Mr. Button's wife is about to have a baby.
   c. Mr. Button is getting ready to go to the doctor's office.
   d. Mr. Button is about to go shopping for new clothes.
   e. Mr. Button is about to be promoted to the president of his company.

2. What kind of tone does the above passage have?
   a. Irate and Belligerent
   b. Sad and Angry
   c. Shameful and Confused
   d. Grateful and Joyous
   e. Nervous and Excited

3. As it is used in the fourth paragraph, the word consecrated most nearly means:
   a. Numbed
   b. Chained
   c. Dedicated
   d. Moved
   e. Exonerated

4. What does the author mean to do by adding the following statement?

   "rubbing his hands together with a washing movement—as all doctors are required to do by the unwritten ethics of their profession."

   a. Suggesting that Mr. Button is tired of the doctor.
   b. Trying to explain the detail of the doctor's profession.
   c. Hinting to readers that the doctor is an unethical man.
   d. Giving readers a visual picture of what the doctor is doing.
   e. Crediting the doctor with authorship of medical ethics guides.

5. Which of the following best describes the development of this passage?
   a. It starts in the middle of a narrative in order to transition smoothly to a conclusion.
   b. It is a chronological narrative from beginning to end.
   c. The sequence of events is backwards—we go from future events to past events.
   d. To introduce the setting of the story and its characters.
   e. To provide a testimonial that leads into a persuasive argument.

6. Which of the following is an example of an imperative sentence?
   a. "Oh, Doctor Keene!"
   b. "Talk sense!"
   c. "Is the child born?"
   d. "Why, yes, I suppose so—"
   e. "What happened?"

7. As it is used in the first paragraph, the word *anachronism* most nearly means:
    a. Comparison
    b. Synecdoche
    c. Aberration
    d. Amelioration
    e. Misplacement

8. This passage can best be described as what type of text?
    a. Expository
    b. Descriptive
    c. Narrative
    d. Persuasive
    e. Technical

9. The main purpose of the first paragraph is:
    a. To explain the setting of the narrative and give information about the story.
    b. To present the thesis so that the audience can determine which points are valid later in the text.
    c. To introduce a counterargument so that the author can refute it in the next paragraph.
    d. To provide a description of the speaker's city and the building in which he works.
    e. To persuade the reader that hospitals are the best places to give birth.

10. The end of the passage implies to the audience that
    a. There is bad weather coming.
    b. The doctor thinks Mr. Button is annoying.
    c. The baby and the mother did not make it through labor.
    d. Something is unusual about the birth of the baby.
    e. Mr. Button lost his job as president of the hardware store.

11. What figurative language is used in the second sentence?
    a. Personification
    b. Metonymy
    c. Simile
    d. Oxymoron
    e. Metaphor

12. In context, the phrase "the This Family and the That Family" is a figure of speech that indicates the Buttons were part of which of the following?
    a. An infamous family tree
    b. Ritzy country club
    c. Unnamed charity organizations
    d. Wealthy Southern heritage
    e. A significant family inheritance

Questions 13–22 are based upon the following passage:

The taxi's radio was tuned to a classical FM broadcast. Janáček's *Sinfonietta*—probably not the ideal music to hear in a taxi caught in traffic. The middle-aged driver didn't seem to be listening very closely, either. With his mouth clamped shut, he stared straight ahead at the endless line of cars stretching out on the elevated expressway, like a veteran fisherman standing in the bow of his boat, reading the ominous confluence of two currents. Aomame settled into the broad back seat, closed her eyes, and listened to the music.

How many people could recognize Janáček's *Sinfonietta* after hearing just the first few bars? Probably somewhere between "very few" and "almost none." But for some reason, Aomame was one of the few who could.

Janáček composed his little symphony in 1926. He originally wrote the opening as a fanfare for a gymnastics festival. Aomame imagined 1926 Czechoslovakia: The First World War had ended, and the country was freed from the long rule of the Hapsburg Dynasty. As they enjoyed the peaceful respite visiting central Europe, people drank Pilsner beer in cafés and manufactured handsome light machine guns. Two years earlier, in utter obscurity, Franz Kafka had left the world behind. Soon Hitler would come out of nowhere and gobble up this beautiful little country in the blink of an eye, but at the time no one knew what hardships lay in store for them. This may be the most important proposition revealed by history: "At the time, no one knew what was coming." Listening to Janáček's music, Aomame imagined the carefree winds sweeping across the plains of Bohemia and thought about the vicissitudes of history.

In 1926 Japan's Taisho Emperor died, and the era name was changed to Showa. It was the beginning of a terrible, dark time in this country, too. The short interlude of modernism and democracy was ending, giving way to fascism.

Aomame loved history as much as she loved sports. She rarely read fiction, but history books could keep her occupied for hours. What she liked about history was the way all its facts were linked with particular dates and places. She did not find it especially difficult to remember historical dates. Even if she did not learn them by rote memorization, once she grasped the relationship of an event to its time and to the events preceding and following it, the date would come to her automatically. In both middle school and high school, she had always gotten the top grade on history exams. It puzzled her to hear someone say he had trouble learning dates. How could something so simple be a problem for anyone?

"Aomame" was her real name. Her grandfather on her father's side came from some little mountain town or village in Fukushima Prefecture, where there were supposedly a number of people who bore the name, written with exactly the same characters as the word for "green peas" and pronounced with the same four syllables, "Ah-oh-mah-meh." She had never been to the place, however. Her father had cut his ties with his family before her birth, just as her mother had done with her own family, so she had never met any of her grandparents. She didn't travel much, but on those rare occasions when she stayed in an unfamiliar city or town, she would always open the hotel's phone book to see if there were any Aomames in the area. She had never found a single one, and whenever she tried and failed, she felt like a lonely castaway on the open sea.

Excerpt from *IQ84* by Haruki Murakami, translated by Jay Rubin, 2011

13. In context, "reading the ominous confluence of two currents" is a metaphor that most nearly represents:
   a. Seeking to catch a fish for dinner
   b. Watching the merging of traffic
   c. Eyeing a wreck on the highway
   d. Enjoying an afternoon drive
   e. Managing a line of cars through a tunnel

14. In relation to the last two paragraphs, the rest of the passage serves primarily to:
   a. Explain why the First World War occurred
   b. Depict a taxi driver at a certain point in history
   c. Engage the reader in an introduction to classical music
   d. Show two characters' inability to socially interact.
   e. Highlight the accuracy and depth of a character's knowledge.

15. The narrator's perspective throughout the passage might be described as that of:
   a. A neutral observer
   b. An intrigued storyteller
   c. An excited historian
   d. A disillusioned journalist
   e. A pedantic professor

16. The statement "Aomame imagined the carefree winds sweeping across the plains of Bohemia" serves as:
   a. Imagery to symbolize the blissful ignorance of the upcoming World War II in Eastern Europe
   b. Simile to denote that our perspective of history is mostly taken for granted
   c. Synecdoche to indicate that the plains and winds stand for bad weather in general
   d. Rhetorical question to call attention to the issue of the upcoming war and its prevention
   e. Personification to indicate that the wind and plains assume human characteristics

17. From the information in the passage, the setting of the story is located in:
   a. Germany
   b. Czech Republic
   c. Japan
   d. Austria
   e. Switzerland

18. Which of the following statements best conveys the effect of these two sentences?

   "As they enjoyed the peaceful respite visiting central Europe, people drank Pilsner beer in cafés and manufactured handsome light machine guns. Two years earlier, in utter obscurity, Franz Kafka had left the world behind."

   a. The adjectives depict the beauty and good fortune of central Europe.
   b. The contrasting tones indicate the period of unrest in the 1920s.
   c. The imagery shows the despondency from World War I.
   d. The interval of time illustrates the contentment of interwar years.
   e. The rambling sentences mimic the confusion of the main character.

19. In the last paragraph, the speaker suggests a way Aomame remembers historical dates, apart from memorization. How would this technique be put into practice?
   a. Writing "Year World War II Ended" on the front of a notecard and the date "1945" on the back of a notecard.
   b. A friend asking you when China joined the World Trade Organization and fact-checking you on your answer by googling the year.
   c. Watching a historical documentary about the Russian Federation and taking notes on a notepad by chronological dates.
   d. Remembering a professor writing the dates on a blackboard regarding the timeline of significant pandemics throughout history.
   e. Recalling that the Treaty of Versailles was signed at the end of World War I and before the interwar period of the 1920s, so it must have occurred somewhere around 1919.

20. What does the word *rote* mean in the passage?
   a. Forceful learning
   b. Learning through context
   c. A large quantity
   d. Creating doubt
   e. Proceeding habitually

21. The author is most likely working on what during this passage?
   a. Counterargument
   b. Setting imagery
   c. Character development
   d. Historical credibility
   e. Implementing a solution

22. The passage ends with a simile that depicts Aomame feeling like a "castaway on the open sea." This simile is referring to what?
   a. Her mother leaving the family when Aomame was young.
   b. The lack of people who are called the same name.
   c. Aomame's father's decision to disconnect from his family.
   d. When the hotels don't have current phone books.
   e. Aomame has to frequently travel alone for her work.

Questions 23–33 are based on the following passage:

2. Chap.

Of their departure Into Holland and their troubls ther aboute, with some of the many difficulties they found and mete withall.

Being thus constrained to leave their native country, their lands and livings, and all their friends and familiar acquaintance, it was much, and thought marvellous by many. But to go into a country they knew not, but by hearsay, where they must learn a new language, and get their livings they knew not how, it being a dear place, and subject to the miseries of war, it was by many thought an adventure almost desperate, a case intolerable, and a misery worse than death; especially seeing they were not acquainted with trades nor traffic, (by which the country doth subsist) but had only been used to a plain country life and the innocent trade of husbandry. But these things did not dismay them, (although they did sometimes trouble them,) for their desires were set on the ways of God, and to enjoy his ordinances. But they rested on his providence, and knew whom they had believed. Yet this was not all. For although they could not stay, yet were they not suffered to go; but the ports and havens were shut against them, so as they were fain to seek secret means of conveyance, and to fee the mariners, and give extraordinary rates for their passages. And yet were they oftentimes betrayed, many of them, and both they and their goods intercepted and surprised, and thereby put to great trouble and charge; of which I will give an instance or two, and omit the rest."

"There was a great company of them purposed to get passage at Boston, in Lincolnshire; and for that end had hired a ship wholly to themselves, and made agreement with the master to be ready at a certain day, and take them and their goods in, at a convenient place, where they accordingly would all attend in readiness. So after long waiting and large expenses, though he kept not the day with them, yet he came at length, and took them in, in the night. And when he had them and their goods aboard, he betrayed them, having beforehand complotted with the searchers and other officers so to do; who took them and put them into open boats, and there rifled and ransacked them, searching them to their shirts for money, yae, even the women, further than became modesty; and then carried them back into the town, and made them a spectacle and wonderment to the multitude, which came flocking on all sides to behold them. Being thus by the catchpole officers riffled and stripped of their money, books and much other goods, they were presented to the magistrates, and messengers sent to inform the Lords of the Council of them; and so they were committed to ward. Indeed the magistrates used them courteously, and showed them what favor they could; but could not deliver them until order came from the Council table. But the issue was, that after a month's imprisonment the greatest part were dismissed, and sent to the places from whence they came; but seven of the principal men were still kept in prison and bound over to the assizes."

In the spring of 1608 another attempt was made to embark and another Dutch shipmaster engaged. This second party assembled at a point between Grimsby and Hull not far from the mouth of the Humber. The women and children arrived in a small bark which became grounded at low water and while some of the men on shore were taken off in the ship's boat they were again apprehended. And to quote again:

"But after the first boat-full was got aboard, and she was ready to go for more, the master espied a great company, both horse and foot, with bills and guns and other weapons: for the country was raised to take them."

"But the poor men which were got on board were in great distress for their wives and children, which they saw thus to be taken, and were left distitute of their helps, and themselves also not having a cloth to shift them with, more than they had on their backs, and some scarce a penny about them, all they had being on the bark. It drew tears from their eyes, and anything they had they would have given to have been on shore again. But all in vain; there was no remedy; they must thus sadly part.

Excerpt from <u>History of Plymouth Plantation</u> by William Bradford, written between 1630 and 1651

23. Which of the following was NOT a difficulty faced by the group of travelers?
    a. They didn't know the new country's language.
    b. They weren't allowed to bring their wives or children to the new country.
    c. They didn't know how to make a living in the new country.
    d. Ships charged exorbitant rates for the voyage to the new country.
    e. They were met with hostility and prejudice by others in their travels.

24. What type of passage is this?
    a. Historical memoir or journal
    b. Passage from a textbook
    c. Poem or Epic Poem
    d. An instructional/technical document
    e. A religious text

25. What went wrong with the ship hired at Boston in Lincoln-shire?
    a. The women got sick due to the rough seas.
    b. The men were separated from their wives and children.
    c. The group couldn't get out of jail in time to board the ship.
    d. The shipmaster betrayed them.
    e. The ship got caught in a storm which caused a shipwreck.

26. Based on the passage, why did the men leave their wives and children?
    a. Armed government officials arrived on the shore.
    b. The government refused to let them out of prison.
    c. The sea was too rough to risk going back for them.
    d. The women were too sick to make the voyage.
    e. The women and children had contracted a disease.

27. Ships charged the group of travelers extra fees because:
    a. they were a vulnerable minority group.
    b. the voyage was particularly long and dangerous.
    c. the government outlawed their departure.
    d. they were wealthy enough to afford it.
    e. the group was so large and rowdy.

28. Based on the passage, which of the following statements BEST describes how the government treated the group of travelers?
    a. The government expelled them from their homeland.
    b. The government persecuted the group due to their different religious beliefs.
    c. The government valued the women and children more than the men.
    d. The government repeatedly tried to stop them from leaving.
    e. The government starved them and kept them from owning property.

29. Which of the following events occurred first?
    a. Some of the group's members were kept in prison and sent to the Assises.
    b. The group became shipwrecked on the shore.
    c. The men cried after getting separated from their wives and children.
    d. The women became sick due to the rough seas.
    e. Government officials embarrassed the group by parading them through town.

30. Which of the following statements best summarizes the second paragraph?
    a. The shipmaster's betrayal led to incredible hardship for the group, including public embarrassment and imprisonment.
    b. The group was imprisoned, and they received better treatment from the magistrates than the lords of the counsel.
    c. The women's sickness led to the government officials discovering, seizing, and imprisoning the group.
    d. While some of the group members were released, others were kept in prison and sent to the Assises.
    e. The women and children make it safely out of town and are met by their husbands shortly afterward.

31. Which of the following statements can reasonably be inferred from the men's reaction at the end of the passage?
    a. The men would have to pay even more exorbitant fees and bribes to bring their wives and children to the commune.
    b. The men were more upset by the loss of their possessions than the separation from their wives and children.
    c. The Dutch shipmaster betrayed them by sailing away instead of attempting to rescue the women and children.
    d. There was a strong likelihood that the men wouldn't see their wives and children for a long time.
    e. The men were overjoyed at having left, even if it meant they were without their wives or children.

32. How did the wives and children become separated from the men?
    a. They were still in prison when the ship set sail.
    b They got sick, forcing their boat to take a detour, and they didn't board the ship in time.
    c. They were on a separate boat, and the captain of their boat betrayed them.
    d. They were pulled off course by strong winds, so they didn't reach the agreed upon meeting place in time.
    e. The wives intentionally left the men so that they could escape with just their children.

33. Which of the following describes why the text is full of confusing grammar/language?
    a. The author is uneducated and does not know how to write very well.
    b. The text was translated from another language and is a poor rendition of the original.
    c. The text is from the 1600s and displays how the English language has changed over time.
    d. The author wrote it while he was a child, so he was not yet a professional writer.
    e. The author wrote it anonymously and changed the spelling and dialect so no one would find out who he was.

Questions 34–44 are based on the following poem. Read it carefully then answer the questions.

> I sit and sew—a useless task it seems,
> My hands grown tired, my head weighed down with dreams—
> The panoply of war, the martial tred of men,
> Grim-faced, stern-eyed, gazing beyond the ken
> Of lesser souls, whose eyes have not seen Death,   5
> Nor learned to hold their lives but as a breath—
> But—I must sit and sew.

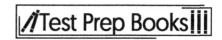

I sit and sew—my heart aches with desire—
That pageant terrible, that fiercely pouring fire
On wasted fields, and writhing grotesque things   10
Once men. My soul in pity flings
Appealing cries, yearning only to go
There in that holocaust of hell, those fields of woe—
But—I must sit and sew.

The little useless seam, the idle patch;   15
Why dream I here beneath my homely thatch,
When there they lie in sodden mud and rain,
Pitifully calling me, the quick ones and the slain?
You need me, Christ! It is no roseate dream
That beckons me—this pretty futile seam,   20
It stifles me—God, must I sit and sew?

Poem "I Sit and Sew" by Alice Moore Dunbar-Nelson, 1918

34. In line 9, the speaker mentions a "pageant." What is she referring to?
   a. A beauty pageant
   b. The current war
   c. A popular play
   d. A wedding celebration
   e. A sewing jubilee

35. In the first stanza, who are the "martial tred of men, / Grim-faced, stern-eyed" that the speaker mentions in lines 3 and 4?
   a. Children
   b. Enemies
   c. Soldiers
   d. Neighbors
   e. Family

36. What idea does the speaker effectively contrast in this poem?
   a. The idea between the usefulness of sewing and the uselessness of war, namely that men's bodies are literally being wasted on the battlefield while sewing gives the opportunity of creating clothes for those same bodies.
   b. The idea between right and wrong, specifically that the war and everything relating to it is immoral, and the domestic side of life, including sewing, can be seen as doing good.
   c. The idea between sacrifice and selfishness; the speaker is admitting that she is being selfish for wanting to pursue her passion of sewing rather than helping out with the war.
   d. The idea between cold and warmth; the speaker contrasts cold and warm imagery and sees the war as something cold and distant and the home as something warm and intimate.
   e. The idea between activeness and passiveness in the sense that the speaker views sewing as passiveness and longs to do something active in order to help out in the war.

37. What type of poetic lines are included in this poem?
    a. English sonnets
    b. Alternating tercets
    c. Rhyming couplets
    d. Syllabic haikus
    e. Iambic trimeter

38. How many stanzas does this poem have?
    a. 1
    b. 2
    c. 3
    d. 4
    e. 5

39. Which of the following line pairs contains an example of internal rhyme?
    a. Lines 5 and 6
    b. Lines 6 and 7
    c. Lines 8 and 9
    d. Lines 9 and 10
    e. Lines 11 and 12

40. In lines 19–20, what does the speaker mean by "roseate dream"?
    a. The speaker had a dream the night before that involved her sister and mother.
    b. The speaker is saying that the dream that calls to her is not cheerful and rosy.
    c. The speaker means that her dreams are warm and rosy while the reality of the war is harsh.
    d. The speaker is saying that her lover calls to her from the battlefield.
    e. The speaker means that her brother died on the battlefield, and thus her dreams have become nightmares.

41. The phrase "My soul in pity flings / Appealing cries" is best understood as
    a. Hyperbole
    b. Simile
    c. Metaphor
    d. Personification
    e. Onomatopoeia

42. In the phrase "Nor learned to hold their lives but as a breath" the speaker is suggesting that
    a. those who have not learned to hold their lives "but as a breath" fail to understand the preciousness of life and its beauty.
    b. she is among those who live their lives "but as a breath" because of the dullness and tediousness of domestic life.
    c. those who live their lives "but as a breath" are not to be envied because they are full of fear and despair.
    d. to live life "but as a breath" means to live a long, exciting life full of surprises and adventures.
    e. she is among those who have not learned to live life as if it could be taken away at any moment.

43. What does the word "thatch" mean in line 16?
    a. sky
    b. moon
    c. roof
    d. rain
    e. bench

44. Which of the following lines contains an example of alliteration?
    a. Line 4
    b. Line 5
    c. Line 11
    d. Line 13
    e. Line 15

Questions 45–55 are based on the following poem. Read it carefully then answer the questions.

Friends, Romans, countrymen, lend me your ears;
I come to bury Caesar, not to praise him.
The evil that men do lives after them;
The good is oft interred with their bones;
So let it be with Caesar. The noble Brutus   5
Hath told you Caesar was ambitious:
If it were so, it was a grievous fault,
And grievously hath Caesar answer'd it.
Here, under leave of Brutus and the rest—
For Brutus is an honourable man;   10
So are they all, all honourable men—
Come I to speak in Caesar's funeral.
He was my friend, faithful and just to me:
But Brutus says he was ambitious;
And Brutus is an honourable man.   15
He hath brought many captives home to Rome
Whose ransoms did the general coffers fill:
Did this in Caesar seem ambitious?
When that the poor have cried, Caesar hath wept:
Ambition should be made of sterner stuff: 20
Yet Brutus says he was ambitious;
And Brutus is an honourable man.
You all did see that on the Lupercal
I thrice presented him a kingly crown,
Which he did thrice refuse: was this ambition?   25
Yet Brutus says he was ambitious;
And, sure, he is an honourable man.
I speak not to disprove what Brutus spoke,
But here I am to speak what I do know.
You all did love him once, not without cause: 30
What cause withholds you then, to mourn for him?
O judgment! thou art fled to brutish beasts,
And men have lost their reason. Bear with me;

85

My heart is in the coffin there with Caesar,
And I must pause till it come back to me.   *35*

An excerpt from <u>Julius Caesar</u> by William Shakespeare, spoken by Marc Antony, 1599

45. This could be considered what type of passage?
    a. Sonnet
    b. Prose
    c. Toast
    d. Speech
    e. Instruction

46. What does the speaker consider his relationship with Caesar to be?
    a. Friendship
    b. Brotherly
    c. Enemies
    d. Paternal
    e. Authoritative

47. What does the speaker say about the good and evil that men do?
    a. The speaker says that men are innately good and learn evil throughout their childhood.
    b. The speaker says that people remember the goodness of someone even after they are dead.
    c. The speaker says that history remembers men's evil deeds and forgets the good that they do.
    d. The speaker says that men do good and evil, but we must not judge them by it.
    e. The speaker says that there are no good men or evil men, just that men have both good and evil in them.

48. The phrase "lend me your ears" is considered which of the following?
    a. Personification
    b. Hyperbole
    c. Simile
    d. Metaphor
    e. Metonymy

49. What is the purpose of the repetition throughout the speech starting in line 10?
    a. Antony is using the repetition to convince the audience that Brutus' honor is something that they cannot deny.
    b. Antony is using the repetition of Brutus being honorable to contrast with Brutus' un-honorable acts to change the audience's perspective of Brutus.
    c. Antony is using the repetition to persuade the audience that although Brutus has done horrible acts, his honor cannot be refuted.
    d. Antony is using the repetition to annoy the audience on purpose because if they start to riot then Antony could possibly escape their tyranny.
    e. Antony is using the repetition to show his audience that the men who killed Caesar should be brought to justice.

50. What proof does Marc Antony offer with the statement that Brutus was an honorable man?
    a. Brutus saved many soldiers in the recent war and brought them back home safely to their families.
    b. Brutus brought home many captives, and their ransoms contributed to the country's finances.
    c. Brutus feeds the hungry and visits orphanages during his spare time.
    d. Brutus captivates the people of Rome by his charismatic personality and eloquent language.
    e. Brutus is concerned with aiding the sick, especially soldiers who are injured from the war.

51. What rhetorical device is used in the line, "Ambition should be made of sterner stuff"?
    a. Imagery
    b. Rhetorical question
    c. Verbal irony
    d. Antithesis
    e. Parallelism

52. Which of the following lines uses pathos to stir the emotions of the audience?
    a. I come to bury Caesar, not to praise him.
    b. And, sure, he is an honourable man.
    c. But here I am to speak what I do know.
    d. When that the poor have cried, Caesar hath wept:
    e. O judgment! thou art fled to brutish beasts,

53. What meter are the lines written in?
    a. Syllabic verse
    b. Anapestic hexameter
    c. Dactylic trimeter
    d. Iambic pentameter
    e. Trochaic tetrameter

54. What is Marc Antony asking of his audience toward the end of the speech?
    a. Antony is asking the audience to throw Brutus and the other conspirators into prison.
    b. Antony is asking the audience to choose a new ruler.
    c. Antony is asking the audience to calm down and stop rioting.
    d. Antony is asking the audience to step up and join the war efforts.
    e. Antony is asking the audience to remember their love for Caesar and to mourn for him.

55. What is the meaning of the last two lines?
    a. Marc Antony is injured and about to die alongside Caesar.
    b. Marc Antony tells the crowd he can no longer stand to speak to them.
    c. Marc Antony left something in the coffin with Caesar and has to go get it.
    d. Marc Antony gets choked up from grief during the speech and has to take a break.
    e. Marc Antony questions Caesar's ambition and requests help from the crowd.

Free-Response Questions

Prompt 1

In the following poem, Robert Frost's "The Road Not Taken," the speaker reflects on making a choice between "two roads." In a well-organized essay, summarize the speaker's dilemma and analyze how the tone, imagery, and metrical language lend meaning to the speaker's thoughts.

> Two roads diverged in a yellow wood,
> And sorry I could not travel both
> And be one traveler, long I stood
> And looked down one as far as I could
> To where it bent in the undergrowth;   5
> Then took the other, as just as fair,
> And having perhaps the better claim,
> Because it was grassy and wanted wear;
> Though as for that the passing there
> Had worn them really about the same,   10
> And both that morning equally lay
> In leaves no step had trodden black.
> Oh, I kept the first for another day!
> Yet knowing how way leads on to way,
> I doubted if I should ever come back.   15
> I shall be telling this with a sigh
> Somewhere ages and ages hence:
> Two roads diverged in a wood, and I—
> I took the one less traveled by,
> And that has made all the difference.   20

Poem "The Road Not Taken" by Robert Frost, 1916

Prompt 2

Read Kate Chopin's "The Story of an Hour." Then write a careful analysis of how the author reveals the character of Mrs. Mallard. Keep in mind the rhetorical strategies that authors use in order to connect to their audience and present their characters (point of view, syntax, tone, figurative language, etc.).

Knowing that Mrs. Mallard was afflicted with heart trouble, great care was taken to break to her as gently as possible the news of her husband's death.

It was her sister Josephine who told her, in broken sentences; veiled hints that revealed in half concealing. Her husband's friend Richards was there, too, near her. It was he who had been in the newspaper office when intelligence of the railroad disaster was received, with Brently Mallard's name leading the list of "killed." He had only taken the time to assure himself of its truth by a second telegram, and had hastened to forestall any less careful, less tender friend in bearing the sad message.

She did not hear the story as many women have heard the same, with a paralyzed inability to accept its significance. She wept at once, with sudden, wild abandonment, in her sister's arms. When the storm of grief had spent itself she went away to her room alone. She would have no one follow her.

There stood, facing the open window, a comfortable, roomy armchair. Into this she sank, pressed down by a physical exhaustion that haunted her body and seemed to reach into her soul.

She could see in the open square before her house the tops of trees that were all aquiver with the new spring life. The delicious breath of rain was in the air. In the street below a peddler was crying his wares. The notes of a distant song which some one was singing reached her faintly, and countless sparrows were twittering in the eaves.

There were patches of blue sky showing here and there through the clouds that had met and piled one above the other in the west facing her window.

She sat with her head thrown back upon the cushion of the chair, quite motionless, except when a sob came up into her throat and shook her, as a child who has cried itself to sleep continues to sob in its dreams.

She was young, with a fair, calm face, whose lines bespoke repression and even a certain strength. But now here was a dull stare in her eyes, whose gaze was fixed away off yonder on one of those patches of blue sky. It was not a glance of reflection, but rather indicated a suspension of intelligent thought.

There was something coming to her and she was waiting for it, fearfully. What was it? She did not know; it was too subtle and elusive to name. But she felt it, creeping out of the sky, reaching toward her through the sounds, the scents, and color that filled the air.

Now her bosom rose and fell tumultuously. She was beginning to recognize this thing that was approaching to possess her, and she was striving to beat it back with her will—as powerless as her two white slender hands would have been. When she abandoned herself a little whispered word escaped her slightly parted lips. She said it over and over under her breath: "free, free, free!" The vacant stare and the look of terror that had followed it went from her eyes. They stayed keen and bright. Her pulses beat fast, and the coursing blood warmed and relaxed every inch of her body.

She did not stop to ask if it were or were not a monstrous joy that held her. A clear and exalted perception enabled her to dismiss the suggestion as trivial. She knew that she would weep again when she saw the kind, tender hands folded in death; the face that had never looked save with love upon her, fixed and gray and dead. But she saw beyond that bitter moment a long procession of years to come that would belong to her absolutely. And she opened and spread her arms out to them in welcome.

There would be no one to live for during those coming years; she would live for herself. There would be no powerful will bending hers in that blind persistence with which men and women believe they have a right to impose a private will upon a fellow-creature. A kind intention or a cruel intention made the act seem no less a crime as she looked upon it in that brief moment of illumination.

And yet she had loved him--sometimes. Often she had not. What did it matter! What could love, the unsolved mystery, count for in the face of this possession of self-assertion which she suddenly recognized as the strongest impulse of her being!

"Free! Body and soul free!" she kept whispering.

Josephine was kneeling before the closed door with her lips to the keyhole, imploring for admission. "Louise, open the door! I beg; open the door--you will make yourself ill. What are you doing, Louise? For heaven's sake open the door."

"Go away. I am not making myself ill." No; she was drinking in a very elixir of life through that open window.

Her fancy was running riot along those days ahead of her. Spring days, and summer days, and all sorts of days that would be her own. She breathed a quick prayer that life might be long. It was only yesterday she had thought with a shudder that life might be long.

She arose at length and opened the door to her sister's importunities. There was a feverish triumph in her eyes, and she carried herself unwittingly like a goddess of Victory. She clasped her sister's waist, and together they descended the stairs. Richards stood waiting for them at the bottom.

Some one was opening the front door with a latchkey. It was Brently Mallard who entered, a little travel-stained, composedly carrying his grip-sack and umbrella. He had been far from the scene of the accident, and did not even know there had been one. He stood amazed at Josephine's piercing cry; at Richards' quick motion to screen him from the view of his wife.

When the doctors came they said she had died of heart disease--of the joy that kills.

Prompt 3

Choose a novel that depicts a dystopian setting. Write an essay in which you analyze the relationship between the characters as they relate to their relationship with the land. Explain how character and setting lends to the meaning of the work.

Avoid plot summary.

You may base your essay on **one** of the following works or choose another of comparable literary quality.

1984	Future Home of the Living God
The Handmaid's Tale	Never Let Me Go
Brave New World	The Road
Fahrenheit 451	Animal Farm
The Giver	The Time Machine
The Core of the Sun	When She Woke
Parable of the Sower	The End We Start From
Station Eleven	Heroes and Villains

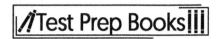

Find Me	*Gold Fame Citrus*
A Clockwork Orange	*V for Vendetta*
Anthem	*A Scanner Darkly*
The Man in the High Castle	*Slaughterhouse-Five*
Who Fears Death	*Brown Girl in the Ring*
The Book of Joan	*The Power*
Do Androids Dream of Electric Sheep	*The Machine Stops*
The Moon is Down	*As I Lay Dying*
Lord of the Flies	*Atlas Shrugged*
Harrison Bergeron	*The White Mountains*

Answer Explanations

1. B: Mr. Button's wife is about to have a baby. The passage begins by giving the reader information about traditional birthing situations. Then, we are told that Mr. and Mrs. Button decide to go against tradition to have their baby in a hospital. The next few passages are dedicated to letting the reader know how Mr. Button dresses and goes to the hospital to welcome his new baby. There is a doctor in this excerpt, as Choice *C* indicates, and Mr. Button does put on clothes, as Choice *D* indicates. However, Mr. Button is not going to the doctor's office nor is he about to go shopping for new clothes. Choice *E* is incorrect; the passage tells us that Mr. Button is already president of his company.

2. E: The tone of the above passage is nervous and excited. We are told in the fourth paragraph that Mr. Button "arose nervously." We also see him running without caution to the doctor to find out about his wife and baby—this indicates his excitement. We also see him stuttering in a nervous yet excited fashion as he asks the doctor if it's a boy or girl.

3. C: Dedicated. Mr. Button is dedicated to the task before him. Choice *A*, numbed, Choice *B*, chained, Choice *D*, moved, and Choice *E*, exonerated, all could grammatically fit in the sentence. However, they are not synonyms with *consecrated* like Choice *C* is.

4. D: Giving readers a visual picture of what the doctor is doing. The author describes a visual image—the doctor rubbing his hands together—first and foremost. The author may be trying to make a comment about the profession; however, the author does not "explain the detail of the doctor's profession" as Choice *B* suggests.

5. D: To introduce the setting of the story and its characters. We know we are being introduced to the setting because we are given the year in the very first paragraph along with the season: "one day in the summer of 1860." This is a classic structure of an introduction of the setting. We are also getting a long explanation of Mr. Button, what his work is, who is related to him, and what his life is like in the third paragraph.

6. B: "Talk sense!" is an example of an imperative sentence. An imperative sentence gives a command. The doctor is commanding Mr. Button to talk sense. Choice *A* is an example of an exclamatory sentence, which expresses excitement. Choices *C* and *E* are examples of interrogative sentences—these types of sentences ask questions. Choice *D* is an example of a declarative sentence. This means that the character is simply making a statement.

7. E: The word *anachronism* most nearly means misplacement. Choice *A*, comparison, is an analogy or similarity to something. Choice *B*, synecdoche, is figurative language wherein a part represents a whole. Choice *C*, *aberration*, means abnormality. Choice *D*, *amelioration*, means improvement.

8. C: This passage can best be described as a narrative, which is a type of passage that tells a story. Choice *A*, expository, is a text organized logically to investigate a problem. Choice *B*, descriptive, is a text that mostly goes about describing something or someone in detail. Choice *D*, persuasive, is a text that is organized as an argument and meant to persuade the audience to do something. Choice *E*, technical, is a text that provides data or information, usually in a STEM field.

9. A: To explain the setting of the narrative and give information about the story. The setting of a narrative is the time and place. We see from the first paragraph that the year is 1860. We also can

discern that it is summer, and Mr. and Mrs. Button are about to have a baby. This tells us both the setting and information about the story.

10. D: Something is unusual about the birth of the baby. The word "curious" is thrown in at the end twice, which tells us the doctor is suspicious about something having to do with the birth of the baby, since that is the most recent event to happen. Mr. Button is acting like a father who is expecting a baby, and the doctor seems confused about something.

11. E: Metaphor is used as figurative language in the second sentence through the term "high gods of medicine." Whether the reference is indicating doctors or other authority figures in healthcare, "high gods of medicine" is a phrase applied to a set of people meant to be taken as a symbol and not as literal truth.

12. D: The phrase "the This Family and the That Family" indicates the Buttons came from a wealthy Southern heritage. The word "heritage" connotes the background belonging to a person, or their ancestry and culture. The original phrase uses capitalization to signify that their family relations, whoever they were, were important people in society.

13. B: The narrator offers a metaphor of the taxi driver as a fisherman. The driver is watching the merging of traffic as a fisherman would watch the merging, or "confluence," of two river currents. The other choices are depictions of actions that aren't represented in the passage.

14. E: In relation to the last two paragraphs, the rest of the passage serves primarily to highlight the accuracy and depth of Aomame's knowledge, specifically of music and history. We see Aomame in the first paragraph, "settled...back," listening to the music while in a taxi. The second, third, and fourth paragraphs depict her detailed knowledge of Janáček's *Sinfonietta*, Czechoslovakia during the First World War, and then Japan around 1926. The last two paragraphs are more about Aomame's personality and family life.

15. B: The narrator's perspective is that of an intrigued storyteller. The passage seems to be an excerpt from a narrative story, and the narrator is certainly intrigued by the main character, Aomame. The narrator describes her actions and thoughts—going into detail about what she loves (history and sport) and her personality and background.

16. A: The statement serves as imagery to symbolize the blissful ignorance of the upcoming World War II in Eastern Europe, as the imagery is followed with Aomame thinking "about the vicissitudes of history," or the downturn of events that World War II brought with it. Using this same imagery, one could say the "carefree winds" turned into a raging storm. The figurative language of simile, synecdoche, rhetorical question, and personification are not represented in the statement.

17. C: The setting of the story is located in Japan. Although Czechoslovakia (former Czech Republic) and Germany are mentioned, we have one context clue that gives us information as to the setting. In the fourth paragraph about Japan, the narrator gives us this statement: "It was the beginning of a terrible, dark time in this country, too." The words "this country" tells us that Japan is the country in which the narrator is telling the story.

18. D: The two sentences are connected by an interval of time that shows the contentment of interwar years: when people in central Europe had the time and resources to drink beer and make weapons; additionally, after Franz Kafka's death but before his work was discovered. Kafka's work is often full of anxiety, isolation, and strained relations, which is also characterized by the literature of the Lost

Generation in the years after World War I. Thus, the text's depiction of time, after the war and before Kafka, is a distinction of peace and contentment.

19. E: The narrator indicates that if Aomame can't remember dates by memorization, she will think of events that happened before and after the specific date she is supposed to remember. Choice *E* is the best depiction of this method, since it determines a date based on events before and after that date.

20. E: The word *rote* means proceeding habitually. In the passage, it is used as an adjective for *memorization*, indicating that learning dates as habitual thought rather than understanding the context around them was a difference between how Aomame learned versus others.

21. C: Out of the available answers, the author is most likely working on character development. The character Aomame is riding in a taxi at the beginning of the passage, and then the passage goes more into depth about her conscious thoughts that form from listening to Janáček's *Sinfonietta*. The passage focuses on showing us who Aomame is by the information she knows and the associations she makes.

22. B: The simile "like a lonely castaway on the open sea" is referring to the lack of people who are called the same name as Aomame. When she gets to hotels while traveling, Aomame will comb through the phone book to see if anyone shares her name, and she feels lonely when she realizes no one in the area is called Aomame.

23. B: The first paragraph explains the difficulties facing the group of travelers. Language and making a living are listed in the second sentence, so Choices *A* and *C* are both incorrect. Extra fees and exorbitant rates are described in the first paragraph's final sentence; therefore, Choice *D* is incorrect. Although the men were later separated from their wives and children, that separation was due to a problem with logistics. There was no prohibition specifically against bringing their wives and children. The entire group was legally barred from leaving the country. Choice *E* is incorrect; we can see how the travelers were treated during their travels, especially in the second paragraph. Thus, Choice *B* is the correct answer.

24. A: We can see that this text records parts of history, so this is most likely a historical memoir or the author's personal journal retelling an event that happened. We see a brief summary of the event before the passage begins.

25. D: The ship hired at Boston in Lincoln-shire is the group's first attempt to flee their homeland, and it's described in the second paragraph. After the group reached an agreement with the shipmaster, he betrayed them to the government, which led to government officials arresting the group. The women didn't become sick or get separated until their second attempt at fleeing, so Choices *A* and *B* are both incorrect. Following the first shipmaster's betrayal, the group did go to jail, but their imprisonment occurred after their first attempt to leave went wrong; therefore, Choice *C* is incorrect. There is no shipwreck in this passage, so Choice *E* is incorrect. Thus, Choice *D* is the correct answer.

26. A: After the men boarded the ship, armed government officials arrived on the shore. Rather than risk everyone getting caught, the Dutch shipmaster raised the anchor, hoisted the sails, and took off. So, even though the men were moved to tears by the separation, there was nothing they could do. The government refused to let some of the group's member out of prison, but that's not what caused the separation; therefore, Choice *B* is incorrect. Choices *C, D,* and *E* are factually incorrect based on the information contained in the third paragraph. Thus, Choice *A* is the correct answer.

27. C: Ships charged the group of travelers extra fees because the government outlawed their departure. The first paragraph says that the government barred them from the ports and havens, so

they needed to find a secret passage out of the country. As helping the group was illegal, ships charged them extra fees in exchange for taking on that risk. The passage doesn't state why the group is being persecuted; therefore, Choice *A* is incorrect. Choice *B* is incorrect because the passage doesn't mention whether the voyage was particularly long or dangerous. While the government does seize property from the group, it's unclear whether the group is particularly wealthy; therefore, Choice *D* is incorrect. Choice *E* is incorrect because nothing is mentioned about the group being rowdy. Thus, Choice *C* is the correct answer.

28. D: The government repeatedly tried to stop the group from leaving. Government officials prohibited the group from entering the ports, arrested the group after their first shipmaster's betrayal, imprisoned the group for attempting to leave, and sent armed soldiers to thwart their second attempt. The government did the opposite of expelling the group; therefore, Choice *A* is incorrect. It's unclear why the government is persecuting the group, so Choices *B* and *E* are incorrect. Although the government does ultimately capture the women and children, it's because they're the only people left on the shore, not because the government values them more; therefore, Choice *C* is incorrect. Thus, Choice *D* is the correct answer.

29. E: Following the first shipmaster's betrayal, the group was arrested, and the government officials paraded them through the street to embarrass them. The group's imprisonment occurred after the embarrassing parade; therefore, Choice *A* is incorrect. A shipwreck never occurred, so Choice *B* is incorrect. The men cried and the women became sick during the group's second attempt at fleeing their homeland. This occurs after the embarrassing parade through town and subsequent imprisonment; therefore, Choices *C* and *D* are both incorrect. Thus, Choice *E* is the correct answer.

30. A: The second paragraph begins with the group reaching an agreement with a shipmaster at Boston in Lincoln-shire. The rest of the paragraph describes the shipmaster's betrayal, government officials parading the group through the town in an embarrassing way, and the group being imprisoned. The group did receive better treatment from the magistrates than the lords of the counsel while in prison, but Choice *B* only describes the end of the paragraph, so it is incorrect. The women don't get sick until the third paragraph; therefore, Choice *C* is incorrect. Choice *D* is incorrect because it only summarizes the second paragraph's last sentence. Choice *E* is not found anywhere in the passage. Thus, Choice *A* is the correct answer.

31. D: At the end of the passage, the men were brought to tears after armed government officials arrested their wives and children. Given that the group had already been imprisoned for attempting to flee their homeland, it's reasonable to infer that their wives and children would receive the same or worse treatment. As such, there was a strong likelihood that the men wouldn't see their wives and children for a long time.

32. B: The wives and children became separated from the men after the women got sick on the way to the meeting place. As a result, the women's boat took a detour, and they weren't ready in time to board the ship before armed government officials arrived on the shore. While some of the group's members were still in prison, many of the wives and children intended to make the voyage; therefore, Choice *A* is incorrect. The captain of the second ship never betrayed them, so Choice *C* is incorrect. The group took a detour due to the women getting sick, not because of strong winds, so Choice *D* is incorrect. Choice *E* is incorrect because the plan was to arrive with the families together and intact. Thus, Choice *B* is the correct answer.

33. C: The text is from the 1600s and displays how the English language has changed over time. Middle English was from 1150 to 1500, so by the time this account was written, the language was slowly changing into Early Modern English, which lasted from the 1540s to about 1650.

34. B: The speaker is referring to the current war, Choice *B*. The lines say: "I set and sew—my heart aches with desire— / That pageant terrible, that fiercely pouring fire / On wasted fields, and writhing grotesque things / Once men" (lines 8–11). Pageant is a metaphor for the battlefield in this poem. After she mentions the word "pageant," the speaker then goes on to describe the "pageant," or war, by describing the fire, fields, and dying men.

35. C: The speaker is referring to soldiers in these lines, so Choice *C* is correct. If we look at the surrounding context clues, the word "war" is mentioned before the description of these men. The word "tred" refers to a sort of weary marching.

36. E: The speaker effectively contrasts the idea between activeness and passiveness in the sense that the speaker views sewing as something passive and longs to do something active in order to help out in the war. Let's look at the poem for proof of this contrast. In the first stanza, the dull act of sewing is set in contrast with the horror that happens in her dreams. In the second stanza, the massacre in the war is contrasted by her, again "sitting and sewing" and yearning to help. Finally, in the third stanza, her "useless seam" is contrasted with the soldiers dying in the mud. The stark contrast of the comforts and ease of sewing to the pain and suffering of soldiers in active duty is a central theme in this poem.

37. C: Poetic lines that can be seen in this poem are rhyming couplets. Rhyming couplets are two pairs of lines that end with rhyming words. We see this all the way through, except for the last line in each stanza, which ends with the word "sew." Here are some examples of the end rhymes of the rhyming couplets: "seems" and "dreams," "things" and "flings," "rain" and "slain."

38. C: A stanza is a group of lines that make up a repeating metrical unit of a poem. We see that there are three stanzas, and each stanza consists of seven lines each. The seven lines have three rhyming couplets (six lines) and end with a seventh line that has no end rhyme. However, the last word in every unit is "sew," which makes a cohesive repetition in the poem.

39. A: The pair of lines that holds an internal rhyme is lines 5 and 6, with the words "eyes" and "lives." Internal rhyme within a poem adds musicality when spoken. It connects the reader to the line before and creates a memorable moment for the reader.

40. B: The speaker is saying that the dream that calls to her is not cheerful and rosy. *Roseate* means rosy, and the speaker says that it is *not* a roseate dream that calls to her. In the poem, it seems as if she feels some sort of duty to the soldiers to go and help, even knowing that what is calling her is the horror of war.

41. D: The phrase "My soul in pity flings / Appealing cries" is best understood as personification. Personification is when something that is not human takes on a human characteristic. In this case, the soul is not human, but it "flings" and "cries" as humans do.

42. E: The speaker is suggesting that she is among those who have not learned to live life as if it could be taken away at any moment. To live life "but as a breath" means that one lives life with the knowledge that life is as brief and as fleeting as a single breath would be. The syntax here is difficult to parse, but we know the speaker is among those who did not learn to live life as a breath, because the line before says: "whose eyes have **not** seen Death, / **Nor** learned to hold their lives but as a breath." The "not/nor"

combination explains that she is among those who have **not** seen death **nor** learned to live life but as a breath.

43. C: The meaning of the word "thatch" is "roof." The context may give some hint; the speaker is inside her home sitting beneath her "thatch." If you are within a home or building, almost always you would be sitting beneath some sort of "roof."

44. D: Line 13 contains an example of alliteration. Alliteration within a poem is when a single line contains two or more uses of a first-letter consonant. For example, in line thirteen we see: "There in that **holocaust** of **hell**, those fields of woe—" The "h" sounds in this line are considered alliteration. Here, the repetition of the "h" sound adds to the intensity of how a war is fought and the horrors that accompany it.

45. D: This passage is considered a speech. This is from Shakespeare's *Julius Caesar*, which was written as a play. This particular scene in the play is when Marc Antony gives a speech in front of a crowd. Choice *A* is incorrect; sonnets have 14 lines and end rhymes, so this is not considered a sonnet. Choice *B* is incorrect. This text is not considered prose because it is metered. The meter is in iambic pentameter. If you say a line out loud, you can hear five "beats" to it. Iambic pentameter is used in plays and poetry. It gives a musical as well as structural quality to speech. Choice *C* is incorrect; this passage is not a toast, but more like a eulogy, since it is spoken in light of someone's death. Choice *E*, instruction, is also incorrect.

46. A: The speaker considers his relationship with Caesar to be a friendship. We see proof of this in line 13: "He was my friend, faithful and just to me." Elsewhere throughout the text, Antony speaks of Caesar as if speaking of a friend, defending him and encouraging the audience to do the same.

47. C: The speaker says that history remembers men's evil deeds and forgets the good that they accomplish. We can see this in lines 3 and 4: "The evil that men do lives after them; / The good is oft interred with their bones." The word "interred" means "buried." Line 3 says that evil "lives on," and we can see this in textbooks or through oral tradition of men who have done brutal things (they are remembered only for those brutal things). Antony tries to display the "good" that Caesar has done throughout this speech and wishes not to bury this remembrance of "goodness" with Caesar's body.

48. E: The phrase "lend me your ears" is considered metonymy. Metonymy is when a word or term is used to stand in for another word or term. For example, when Antony says "lend me your ears," he means "lend me your hearing," or, "listen to me." "Ears" is substituted for "hearing," which makes this a use of metonymy.

49. B: Antony is using the repetition of Brutus being honorable to contrast with Brutus' un-honorable acts to change the audience's mind. A touch of verbal irony is being used in this repetition, as Brutus' conspiracy against and murder of Caesar was anything but honorable. Marc Antony uses this repetition almost as a taunt to the audience. The more Antony calls Brutus "honorable," the less Brutus seems so, especially with the progression of the speech.

50. B: Brutus brought home many captives, and their ransoms contributed to the country's finances. This is mentioned in lines 16 and 17: "He hath brought many captives home to Rome / Whose ransoms did the general coffers fill." The other answer choices are not mentioned in the passage.

51. C: Verbal irony is used in the line "Ambition should be made of sterner stuff." Verbal irony is closely related to sarcasm. It is when the speaker expresses one thing but means the opposite. When Antony says "Ambition should be made of sterner stuff," he is, in a way, mocking the enemies of Caesar by saying, if Caesar is "ambitious" because he weeps when the poor cry, then ambition should be "made of sterner stuff." Antony is trying to prove that Caesar did **not** act with ambition as his enemies say he did.

52. D: The line that uses significant pathos to stir the emotions of the audience is Choice *D*: "When that the poor have cried, Caesar hath wept." Antony is using this line to show that Caesar was always on the side of the Roman people and that he could and did empathize with them. Antony is hoping that Caesar's show of empathy will in turn evoke empathy for Caesar from the crowd. Remember that **pathos** is the rhetorical device that invokes emotion from the audience, often pulling at their hearts.

53. D: These lines are written in iambic pentameter. Iambic pentameter is the meter that Shakespearian plays are written in because the meter works well with the English language, giving it five "beats," or stresses, and taking away from the sing-song iambic tetrameter (four beats per line, often found in nursery rhymes). Iambic pentameter is a popular meter for epic poems, dramas, sonnets, and many other poetic forms.

54. E: Antony is asking the audience to remember their love for Caesar and to mourn for him. In lines 30 and 31, he says this: "You all did love him once, not without cause: / What cause withholds you then, to mourn for him?" Antony is asking why the crowd refuses to mourn for Caesar so that they will ask themselves the same thing. He is hoping the audience will see through Brutus' speech and join Antony in mourning for Caesar, potentially even seeking justice for his death.

55. D: Marc Antony gets choked up from grief during the speech and has to take a break. The two lines are this: "My heart is in the coffin there with Caesar, / And I must pause till it come back to me." By his heart being in the coffin, he means that he is grieving for the death of his friend. He says he must "pause" until his heart "comes back," which means that he must stop talking until he can regain his composure to speak again.

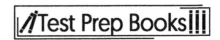

Dear AP Test Taker,

We would like to start by thanking you for purchasing this study guide for your AP English Literature and Composition exam. We hope that we exceeded your expectations.

Our goal in creating this study guide was to cover all of the topics that you will see on the test. We also strove to make our practice questions as similar as possible to what you will encounter on test day. With that being said, if you found something that you feel was not up to your standards, please send us an email and let us know.

We would also like to let you know about other books in our catalog that may interest you.

Test Name	Amazon Link
AP Biology	amazon.com/dp/1628456221
AP Chemistry	amazon.com/dp/1628457090
AP Comparative Government	amazon.com/dp/1628456388
AP English Language & Composition	amazon.com/dp/162845508X

We have study guides in a wide variety of fields. If the one you are looking for isn't listed above, then try searching for it on Amazon or send us an email.

Thanks Again and Happy Testing!
Product Development Team
info@studyguideteam.com

FREE Test Taking Tips DVD Offer

To help us better serve you, we have developed a Test Taking Tips DVD that we would like to give you for FREE. **This DVD covers world-class test taking tips that you can use to be even more successful when you are taking your test.**

All that we ask is that you email us your feedback about your study guide. Please let us know what you thought about it – whether that is good, bad or indifferent.

To get your **FREE Test Taking Tips DVD**, email freedvd@studyguideteam.com with "FREE DVD" in the subject line and the following information in the body of the email:

 a. The title of your study guide.

 b. Your product rating on a scale of 1-5, with 5 being the highest rating.

 c. Your feedback about the study guide. What did you think of it?

 d. Your full name and shipping address to send your free DVD.

If you have any questions or concerns, please don't hesitate to contact us at freedvd@studyguideteam.com.

Thanks again!

Made in the USA
Coppell, TX
03 September 2021